HOW THEY MADE IT

How They Made It: Secrets from Successful Entrepreneurs You've Never Heard of (But Should)

This book is set in the typeface *Athelas* designed by Veronika Burian and Jose Scaglione.

Cover design by Yvonne Parks | PearCreative.Ca
Author Photo by Orser Studio

Paperback ISBN: 978-1-955546-39-3
Hardcover ISBN: 978-1-955546-44-7

A Publication of *Tall Pine Books*
119 E Center Street, Suite B4A | Warsaw, Indiana 46580
www. Tallpinebooks. Com

| 1 23 23 20 16 02 |

Published in the United States of America

HOW THEY MADE IT

SECRETS FROM SUCCESSFUL ENTREPRENEURS YOU'VE NEVER HEARD OF (BUT SHOULD)

PATRICK O'MEARA

I dedicate this book to my wife, Rosella. You stood by me and encouraged me throughout all of my highs and lows. Navigating life with me over the last thirty-seven years is not for the faint at heart and you never stopped believing in me. When I was in my darkest most vulnerable place, you guarded me like a lioness and fought for me to come back stronger than ever. You are my hero.

CONTENTS

INTRODUCTION

FOR THIRTY-THREE YEARS, I have had the privilege of being a trusted advisor to C-Suite leaders as it relates to the art of the possible in transforming areas of their companies. I have had the opportunity to work with some of the brightest and most intuitive people in the world. I've also had a front row seat in seeing firsthand what works and what doesn't work when it comes to key growth and breakthrough moments for individuals and companies. On March 13, 2020, while serving a client as a Senior Partner in a global consulting and technology company, I had no idea that so many significant things were going to come to a screeching halt. I was on my way back from my client meeting in Dallas and all of my news feeds were announcing that everything was shutting down due to the COVID pandemic. Quarantines, masks, reducing group gatherings, not being able to visit people in the hospital, etc. seemed to rain down on society globally all at once. I went from traveling over forty weeks out of the year, working with clients on their business transformation initiatives, to everything stopping all at once. If that wasn't enough, race issues broke out in the US in an unprecedented way and riots broke out in many cities with a vengeance. It seemed as though everything in society was pulling apart at the seams with no end in sight. After several months, my routine was officially broken, and significant disruptions continued to hit the marketplace without relief. As a result of this, I started to seek a new normal, a place where I could make sense of what was happening. I began thinking through some of the different global disruptions that had impacted my career over the last thirty-three years. I remembered the Desert Storm War in 1991, the horrific attack on the US on September 11, 2001, the tremendous economic downturn that came about in 2007 and 2008 with the eventual bankruptcy of General Motors (GM) on June 1, 2009—something that no one thought was possible. GM wasn't the only impacted company. Bankruptcies ripped across every sector of the US, hitting the housing markets and financial institutions especially hard.

Even though I had all of these experiences and watched things rebound, nothing seemed to prepare me for what was happening in the world around me. I started reviewing key things that my mentors had told me throughout the years based on their accumulated wisdom from the past, and then I began reflecting on my career and remembering key entrepreneurs that I used as inspiration to help me grow as a business leader.

I started my career in 1990 in Detroit selling and program managing custom software development, consulting, and technology solutions for global clients in the automotive industry. My eyes opened wide as I saw leaders in small, medium, and large companies standing for something bigger than themselves. I saw their driving passion to invent, innovate, and contribute to marketplace initiatives that had never been brought to life. I saw creativity oozing out of Detroit in order to help bring world-class solutions to the market. They wanted to add significant value to the world. They wanted to make their mark and change the world for the better. As I watched and admired those marketplace leaders in the corporate setting that surrounded me, I was also drawn to watch and learn from entrepreneurs in my community. Business owners that brought ideas to the market from scratch or those that stewarded family-owned businesses over decades and sometimes over generations. These entrepreneurs had the ability to see key things that added value, with a compelling passion and creative capability to bring their inventions and innovations to the market and win. There was a fearlessness in them that inspired me. As I started paying attention to their lives and their stories, I saw myself being challenged to be more entrepreneurial myself, more value centered, and more results oriented in my personal and professional life. In the turbulent times that surrounded me, I started to feel some solace in meditating on the lives of these entrepreneurs. I looked up the definition of "entrepreneur." In Meriam Webster's Dictionary, I saw that it means "one who organizes, manages, and assumes the risks of a business or enterprise." Not only are these individuals smart, creative, and resilient, they are doing it while taking responsibility for the operations, management, and complete financial risk of the endeavor. In my corporate role, I managed some of these things, but not all of them in their entirety. During this time of reflection, my respect for these entrepreneurs grew and I decided to write about them, to not only inspire me in these difficult times, but to also inspire you and help us all keep moving forward. In the first section of this book, I feature the entrepreneurial journeys of five very interesting individuals and teams. I will help bring out 1) where they came from, 2) how they got started, 3) what their key challenges were, 4) how they broke through, and 5) what's next for them in the future. I then share entrepreneurial insights that will help you see what strengths, mindsets, values, and behaviors helped them to succeed.

You will learn about: John McMullen, a man born into poverty in Flint, Michigan, who rose to found and lead one of the most successful GM dealer groups in the US.

Puja Bhattacharya and Dilpreet Chadha who were unexpectedly laid off in the spring of 2020 to rise up, start, and run a successful all-woman global company.

Chris Borroni-Bird, a Cambridge PhD physicist that originally patented the chassis skateboard concept for electric vehicles who has now founded his own mobility company to bring solutions to the poorest of the poor.

Sarah Schneider, an extremely creative individual that founded The Fed Community Restaurant with her husband James based on a vision to transform a historic building and make it a place where friends, family, and loved ones can share special moments together.

Darris Stoll, a third-generation servant leader who worked with their expert team to transform Stoll Industries by bringing new products and concepts forward during very turbulent times.

The second section of this book includes "Your 21-Word Growth Challenge," which features twenty-one qualities these entrepreneurs demonstrate corporately. Each quality contains a practical rubric for personal evaluation and inspiration for your own growth journey.

I believe that reading these stories will impact your professional and personal life. My hope is that you will find yourself in one of these stories, and that it will motivate you to get on a course to bring a part of who you are, in whatever role you have, into the marketplace and change the world. With all the market, social, and political pressures that are raging today, having a clear vision for what contributes to a person breaking through and succeeding is more important than ever.

SECTION ONE

THE STORIES

CHAPTER ONE

UNSTOPPABLE DRIVE TOWARD SUCCESS

The John B. McMullen Story

THERE ARE PEOPLE who grow up in poverty and have extremely humble beginnings. For many, these circumstances shape how they see themselves—defeated and never able to get ahead. For others, they discover a burning ember of significance, a drive to succeed, a knowing that they were created for something more, something special. Discovering that significance provides determination and strength to push through hardships into success.

All entrepreneurs have a drive to succeed. This is basic, but if it doesn't run deep, it won't bear fruit over the long haul. It's not something that they need to conjure up; it's something that they rely on when no one sees what they see. It's something that pulls them out of dark places when nothing seems to be going their way. John McMullen's story represents a fantastic example of an unstoppable drive toward success. He starts with nothing and without exception takes advantage of every opportunity that comes in front of him. As he strives for excellence, he puts trusted people around him which extends his reach and impact. He perfects his timing to get in and out of deals at the right time, and he never loses sight of his humble beginnings. Most of all, he gives of himself and his resources to strengthen others.

BACKGROUND AND PERSONAL HISTORY

John was born in 1928 and was raised in Flint, Michigan, during the Depression. He and his family basically had nothing. They lived at the back of a lot with outside toilets, and they had to carry their water to the house. John had three sisters, and his father worked for the Welfare Department. To supplement food stamps, which was their means of survival, his father created a garden that helped to supply the right kind of food and nutrition to the family. As time went on, the city brought water and sewer down the street, so they moved to a house forward on the lot and hooked up to water and sewer, which was a thrill for the family.

John eventually attended Northern High School in Flint. To help support the family, when he was fourteen, he worked at the corner store and gas station and helped pump gas. He remembers it being tough times as food and gas rationing was in place. After John graduated from high school, he landed a job at the Arctic Sealtest Dairy. Sealtest sent John to Michigan State University to get some further training on pasteurizing milk and being an overall dairyman. John was 100 percent committed to the dairy business and believed that he could make a good living at it. He worked in the plant at first to help process the milk. He then ended up doing everything, including helping shoe and feed the horses, wash the bottles, bottle the milk, and stack and load the milk for deliveries. His primary job eventually became a milk delivery man serving the local neighborhoods via horse-drawn carriage. He had done every job in the dairy process and had an appetite to experience how all of the jobs fit together. It's not every day that a person grasps the entire process of the work environment and its associated value. John's training in this area, and his focus on operational excellence, would become a key differentiator for him in the future. John worked long and hard six to seven days a week from before sunrise to after sunset. During those hard times, John started to notice that some of his customers would have a note on the bottle that said, "Gone north. No milk today." He couldn't imagine how anyone in those times could take off work and "Go north." He'd think, *How do they do that?* He wanted to know what they did for a living and what kind of job would give them that kind of freedom. John had never avoided hard work. He wasn't looking for an easier life. He saw that others were prospering, and he wanted to put himself in a position to prosper and gain freedom beyond what he had seen growing up and what he was experiencing at that time. One night while out bowling for recreation with his team, John saw a glimmer of hope. He saw a guy come in, take off his tie and his suit coat, and start to bowl. His name was Whitey Bazinski. In those hard times, Whitey represented success in John's eyes, so he went up to Whitey and said, "What do you do for a living?"He said, "I sell cars."John said, "Well, do you make good money?"

"Oh, yeah," Whitey said. That impressed John, because he was working all of those long days and thought that maybe he could sell cars, too, and make a better life for himself.

STARTING IN BUSINESS

Soon after that, in 1951 at the age of twenty-three, John went to Summerfield Chevrolet in Flint. Arthur Summerfield had opened the dealership in 1929 and by 1953 it had become one of the largest Chevrolet dealerships in Michigan. Arthur Summerfield was appointed the Postmaster General under President Eisenhower in 1953 and remained in that role until 1961. During that time, his son Bud Summerfield ran the dealership.

John walked in the front door of the dealership and asked the receptionist, "Who do I see to get a job?" She said, "What kind of job are you looking for?"

"A salesman," John said.

"Well, you will need to talk with Bud Summerfield." Just as she spoke those words, Bud walked down the stairway from the second floor. John approached Bud and asked him if there was any chance of talking to him about selling cars. Bud looked at John and asked, "What makes you think you can sell cars?"

John replied, "Well, I load a milk truck up in the morning before daylight. I work until after dark, and I think that if I work that hard selling cars, I should be able to make a living."

Bud said, "Well, come on upstairs." They talked for a while and then Bud brought in his sales manager and his truck manager, and they decided to give him a try. John gave his notice at the dairy soon after that. But John had no money. His first two weeks, he didn't sell a car. He got his first paycheck and it said $0.00. He thought, *What have I gotten myself into?* He decided to go to the Household Finance Department and borrow $25 to buy some food and basic staples. John said, "The next week I did sell my first car and then it just started." He sold a few more cars and the momentum never stopped! John had found his place in business. John's work ethic was stellar at the dealership. He came in early and stayed late every day. He learned his job and became excellent at it. He familiarized himself with the operations of the dealership, and like in the dairy business, became familiar with every department and how everything worked together to add value to the overall business. With this attention to detail and excellent execution in his role, he removed any question in Summerfield's mind that John would be a strong candidate for promotion. One year later, John was promoted to assistant manager, and shortly after that, at the age of 26 in 1954, he became the sales manager of new cars. He eventually became the general manager of the dealership and stayed in that role until 1965 at the age of 37. Under John's leadership, Summerfield Chevrolet went from being one of the top ten dealerships in Michigan to becoming one of the top ten dealerships in the country!

KEY CHALLENGES AND BREAKTHROUGH

Having such personal success, John made a bold move in 1965 and notified Summerfield that he wanted to become a dealer himself. Summerfield said that he couldn't help John financially, but that he could certainly give a good recommendation of John to Chevrolet. Chevrolet in turn notified Bill Ross, the general manager of Pontiac Motors. Ross was very interested in John because of his performance and because Summerfield had become such a great success. When John had his initial meeting with Pontiac Motors, Ross said that John needed to run a larger operation based on his experience and successful track record. He asked John if he would consider working for Frank Audette. Frank was a very strong and accomplished businessman, but he didn't have John's experience running a dealership, so it looked like a good partnership potential for both of them. John quickly responded that he would consider it only if he owned part of the dealership. Based on this discussion, a meeting was set up at the Kingsley Inn in Bloomfield Hills, Michigan. John and Frank got along really well, and they discussed having John come on board to lead the effort. John was very direct and said that he didn't want to be part of it unless he could buy into the dealership. Frank responded by saying that he couldn't sell him any stock in the company. John said, "Well, then I am not interested."The meeting broke up shortly after, and John thought he would need to find a different way forward to fulfill his dream of owning his own dealership. He knew that Frank was offering him a great deal, but it didn't fit within his plan. He didn't know what the next step was going to be, and he knew that he had to hold out for his dream of ownership and not compromise. He was scared to death that he made the wrong decision, but he battled the fear and stood his ground.

A few days later, John got a call from Ross saying that Frank wanted to meet again. In that meeting, Frank offered John a maximum of 25 percent of the company. John accepted, but at that time, only had enough for a 10 percent stake. He took all the money that he had ($30,000) and purchased the 10 percent stake in the dealership. He quit his job at Summerfield's and went all in. Initially, he had to borrow money to support all his living expenses, including buying groceries. As he looks back at it now, he sees that it was one of the gutsiest moves that he ever made. That decision to lay it all on the line provided the breakthrough that he was looking for. It also created a strategic building block that changed John's destiny as a businessman. John stepped into a whole new level of impact and exposure, not only to the local business community, but to the leadership of General Motors. John became an owner. This put him in a tremendous position to influence the businesses that he would lead, but it also opened doors that he never thought possible. Because he had confidence in what he had accomplished to date, took courage to fight for a chance to become an owner, and wasn't overcome by fear, this moment in his life put John on an upward trajectory that hasn't stopped. They moved forward in 1966 with the deal and the dealership was called Audette Pontiac in Troy, Michigan. The dealership opened with the 1967 model. The dealership did extremely well and Pontiac Motors was very excited.

SCOPE AND IMPACT

Since John was leading such a successful operation, Pontiac reached out to him again to open a dealership in Pontiac, Michigan. They had a retail store there at the time, but they wanted to do away with it and open a full dealership operation. John let Pontiac know that he needed to check with Frank Audette. Frank was okay with the deal as long as John could back fill his role at the dealership in Troy. Frank Audette became John's partner again in 1970 for this new venture understanding that once the dealership got going, John would buy him out and he'd own 100 percent in McMullen Pontiac in Pontiac, Michigan. McMullen Pontiac became very successful, and John expanded into two more dealership locations in 1974 and 1975 in and around Lansing, Michigan. Also, at that time, Frank Audette was looking to move out of the Pontiac brand and transition into selling the Cadillac brand. In those days, you couldn't have both brands under one owner, so John offered to buy Frank out in 1975. John did buy Frank out and renamed the Audette Pontiac dealership to Somerset Pontiac in Troy, Michigan. With this momentum, Pontiac Motors came to John with another opportunity in Port Richey, Florida. John was interested and said that he'd fly down to the area and check it out. He met with the Pontiac sales manager of that zone, which was on Highway 19 where there was nothing except for a few buildings. John said, "You want me to put a dealership here?" The Pontiac sales manager said that based on their research, this was going to be a growth area. Based on Pontiac's guidance, John took a leap of faith, found a piece of property, and went to the bank to finance the building. The bank agreed once they understood John's track record and heard John's vision for the property. Not too long after the establishment of this dealership in 1986, John purchased a second Florida dealership in 1988 in Clearwater. As John continued in his successful string of dealerships in Michigan and Florida, he was also spending quality time with key General Motors leaders like Pete Estes, president of General Motors from 1974 to 1981; Jim McDonald, president and COO of General Motors from 1981 to 1987; and John DeLorean, the youngest General Motors division head that developed the Pontiac GTO, Pontiac Firebird, and Pontiac Grand Prix muscle cars, and who went on to establish the DeLorean Motor Company. They would play golf, as well as other leisure activities, to exchange ideas. John became the president of the Pontiac Dealers Association in Detroit for a couple of years and was heavily involved in the National Automotive Dealer Association (NADA) and the Michigan Automotive Dealer Association (MADA). John was sought after because of his track record, but also because of his approach to success. John served on the board of the International Auto Show in Detroit for several years and worked hard to be involved in that activity as much as he could. He received a very prestigious honor to also serve on the GM President's Board. This was a very high honor as dealers that were top ten volume producers in the country were asked to participate. Not only was this a great experience, but it also gave John invaluable networking connections and exposure.

John established a winning approach to setting up dealerships and having each one become very successful. This is obvious based on what he accomplished in the marketplace and the respect that he earned from the top GM leaders. John had an inherent drive to do something better than what his father and his family had accomplished. This wasn't out of ego, but a sincere desire to provide a better life for himself, his parents, and his sisters. Jim McDonald asked John to speak to the sons and daughters of dealers at an annual meeting on how to win in the auto world. John also had an opportunity to speak to the General Motors Institute on how to be successful in the auto business. In both settings, John explained that it's very easy to be successful in the auto business: you just have to surround yourself with good people.

As John became more successful, it stretched him and caused him to contemplate whether he wanted to keep expanding with more dealerships or diversify into other areas. During this time, John experienced a very impactful situation where one of his top people at a dealership broke his trust in a significant way. He was already stretched as he would spend two to three days at each location in order to observe the flow of the operation. If he expanded, he would need to find more trusted team members that could help him grow. At this juncture, however, John decided to make a decision for himself and his family and optimize his dealership portfolio and begin to look to diversify into other areas. Some of the areas were personal and some of them involved investments.

Soon after coming to the decision to optimize his portfolio, John sold his two dealerships in Florida and sold the McMullen dealerships in Pontiac and Lansing. John completed this transition in 1991 and was 63 years old. John retained ownership of Somerset in Troy until he sold it in 2019 at the age of 91. John wanted to have one key location that he could oversee to stay in the business, and it also served as his headquarters for the other interests that he wanted to pursue. During John's career, he also amassed one of the most prestigious antique luxury car collections in the world: 140 cars that earned the respect of the most experienced car collectors. RM Auctions, Inc. put a book together to feature John's cars for the auction, which took place on June 9, 2007. This is what they had to say about his collection:The collection of Mr. John McMullen is like no other, representing decades of automotive history as well as marquees that changed the face of American motoring. Over the years, we have watched as John McMullen's dedication to collecting important, top quality motor cars has served to create an assemblage that exemplifies perfection, with many examples having scored 100 points in judging and capturing numerous awards at concours events across the country. The McMullen collection offers rarity, excellence, and provenance in each and every car. It is a peerless group of motor cars in terms of quality and presentation.

After the auction was over, John had sold 80 percent of the collection for a significant profit, which brought his overall collection to a place that was more manageable for him moving forward.

ENTREPRENEURIAL INSIGHTS

As I reflect on John's story, there are four key elements that come to life for me: respect, valuing each team member, being an extravagant giver, and impeccable timing. (Note that you will find each characteristic from all the Entrepreneurial Insights sections featured in section 2 of this book. The word as it is used in section 2 and its numeric order is listed in parentheses.)

RESPECTED (1-RESPECT)

John has a gentle way about him that disarms, but it is partnered with a passion and a drive for excellence that makes you respect him instantly. It's not something that he tells you that makes you respect him, it's who he is. His presence is kind, and his drive is infectious. I think that he commanded the respect and admiration of General Motors' senior leaders, bankers, and community leaders in the market because of what he brought to the table: an authentic drive and desire to see people win, just as he was winning. He associates with people that have experience and potential, but he also has a strong desire, for himself and for others, to develop into something more for themselves and for their families. I believe that these deep beliefs cause people around him to respect him and the things that are important to him.

VALUES EACH TEAM MEMBER (2-TEAM)

Broadly speaking, there are two ends of the spectrum for leaders today. One end cares only about results and sees people as expendable. The result of this drives fear and intimidation into the organization as a source of motivation. The other end of the spectrum cares about the entire person and the healthy culture of the team. This leader is willing to invest everything that they have into their team, but with the expectation that they will contribute in a significant way. The result of this drives trust, high expectations, accountability, and transparency into the organization. This is John's style of leadership. John has a glimmer in his eye when he talks about the significance of the team that he surrounds himself with. John considers himself very lucky to be able to spot people. I actually think that it is a genuine gift, especially after he demonstrated the ability to pick great people throughout his career. I think also people that are looking for the best leaders to work for spot John as a prime target to learn from and be mentored by. John made a lot of his decisions on hiring people based on how successful they were at managing things at home:

Is their family in good shape and functioning well? Are they overcoming adversity in a constructive way? Where did they come from? What have they accomplished, and where do they want to go in life? How is their marriage going?How are their kids doing? Do they have good morals? Are they honest? Do they have a good reputation? John knew from growing up in the Depression that a strong home life produced a stable and healthy environment to grow, especially in difficult times. John had that growing up and he wanted to see the same thing on his team. John wanted team members to understand that they had to be willing to sacrifice in order to attain their goals. Just as he was willing to sacrifice temporal frills in order to gain momentum for the future, he wanted his team members to be focused and dedicated to the same principle.

LIFELONG EXTRAVAGANT GIVER (3-GIVER)

John has a great appreciation for the success that he has had in the marketplace, especially feeling very fortunate to have been able to rise out of the tough times of the Depression and make his mark on the world. With this came a big heart to serve those that were in need. Throughout his career, he has been active in the community by providing financially, and being personally involved, in supporting blood and cancer drives. He was on the board of St. Joseph's Hospital in Pontiac, Michigan, and helped financially with the expansions at the McLaren Hospital in Lapeer, Michigan. Though John is uncomfortable talking about it, he continues to this day, helping friends and family members that he sees as deserving people that have fallen on hard times. John said, "Sometimes people work hard and are doing all the right things, but they have a rough go of it. In that situation, I've helped them get through it." In business deals, where John says that a person had worked hard and was doing all the right things, but lacked capital, he would make it available to them. He said, "Sometimes people just need a little help, and I want to be there for them. I've helped a lot of families that got on hard times due to illness, accidents, and things like that. I have sort of became a father to them to pull them through those hardships."

TIMING IS EVERYTHING (4-TIMING)

In talking with John about his story, it is clear that he has an impeccable track record for timing. He says that it's something in his gut. I'm sure that that is true. I also see in John a continued focus on operational excellence to this day. He surrounds himself with great team members. John is a comprehensive listener and is able to absorb, process, and simplify complex problems. Whatever the secret is, John has a gift to get in and get out of investments at the right time. He recalls getting a break at Summerfield to become the sales manager, meeting Frank Audette at the right time, buying and selling his dealerships at the right time, buying and selling a large portion of his automobile collection at the right time, and, yes, buying and selling property at the right time. Many successful entrepreneurs have these qualities, but I know very few who have done it consistently over a lifetime. Even at the age of ninety-four, when you look into John's eyes, you see a man that is ready for an adventure. Before I met John, one of his best friends told me that he hopes to be just like him when he's ninety-three. After spending time with John, I understand why he has this sincere hope. I now have it, too.

CHAPTER TWO

RESILIENT RESTART

The Puja Bhattacharya and Dilpreet Chadha Story

PEOPLE GO TO work on what seems like a normal day, doing a fantastic job and contributing significant value to the company that they work for, only to find out that their world has suddenly changed. As the company makes tough decisions to downsize due to very difficult market conditions, they find that they no longer have a job. They are suddenly forced to work through the emotions of disappointment and disbelief. For some, as they work through the fog of emotions, a resilience can rise within them to overcome... to restart! They begin to remind themselves of the passion that drew them into their field of expertise in the first place. They reflect on what drove them to excellence each day that they worked for the company. They dig deep with purpose and courage and decide to start a business in their field of expertise and forge a vision of their own into the marketplace.

Puja Bhattacharya and Dilpreet Chadha have done exactly this. After being separated from their employment due to corporate downsizing events, they decided to form a partnership and took on a resilient restart of their own in India at the beginning of the COVID pandemic. When so many unknowns were in front of them, not only did they start a new business, in their first year they provided business research and talent intelligence services on three continents with a highly educated and experienced all-woman team. They provide excellent value to global clients while giving other women, who have also been displaced by market circumstances, an opportunity to excel in their careers while working remotely and supporting their families.

HISTORY AND PERSONAL BACKGROUND

Puja is from Kolkata (Calcutta) and is a Bengali. When she was just five years old, her father, an officer in the Indian Air Force, died suddenly of a cardiac arrest. Reeling from this sudden change, she was too young to understand all that was happening to her. What she did see is that she, her mother and her two-year-old sister were now on their own. In the midst of all the changes, they had to relocate from Bangalore where her father was posted back to Kolkata, their hometown. Puja's mom had to start a new life and go from being a homemaker to becoming the wage earner for their home. She had a background in chemistry and became a chemistry teacher in a nearby school. When this shift took place, Puja took responsibility for much of the home so that her mom could work and provide for them. It was a very heavy responsibility that made her childhood very difficult. In the back of her mind, she carried the fact that she had lost her father. What would happen if something happened to her mother? Even though Puja carried this burden, she is grateful for several positive things that came out of her early experiences. The first was that her circumstances forced a sense of responsibility on her at a very early age. She saw the value and fruit of dedicating herself to support the care and well-being of her family. Secondly, she always saw her mother working hard to provide for the family without reservation and with much sacrifice. Her mother became a role model of independence to her to become financially independent. As a result of her mother's example, their family of three never faced financial hardships of any kind.

Thirdly, her mother never complained and made sure that Puja and her sister never let anyone call them poor kids for losing their father or let them feel sorry for themselves for their difficult times. Fourthly, it molded Puja into a very compassionate person for those suffering with difficult or unfortunate circumstances. Learning from these experiences created a strong self-respect—a confidence and desire to stand strong as an independent person.

Puja completed her undergraduate and postgraduate work in economics from the University of Kolkata and attained her Master in Business Administration (MBA) from Symbiosis Institute of Management Studies, Pune. Soon after graduating with her MBA in 2006, she joined a company that provided knowledge process outsourcing (KPO). It was a very new concept in India at the time and it gave Puja excellent experience and insights into working with consulting firms and other large organizations. After working there for a year, she joined a world-class HR consulting firm that provided rewards and compensation services to companies in every region of the world. Puja joined with the excitement of knowing that she could work with a team to set up the first business research arm of the company.

Dilpreet comes from Delhi, the northern part of India, and is part of a Shik family. She has spent her entire life in the capital city. She grew up in a very stable home environment with her mother, father, and older brother. In her home, and with her extended family, the focus for the future was not on higher education. The men were expected to join the family businesses and the women were expected to get married and start a family. In Dilpreet's case, however, she was always academically strong and had a desire to continue her education and have a career of her own. Confronting the traditions of her family was very difficult because no one in her family had respectfully challenged "how things were always done." Her family was full of love, but she knew that she needed to find a way to respectfully challenge the status quo and break out of the family traditions that were threatening her dreams. She decided to let her grades and academic accomplishments over time speak for themselves. As she was finishing her twelfth year, her scores were very high, and her mother took notice of that. Her mother became her advocate and helped align her father with her desires to pursue her undergraduate degree. With everyone in agreement, Dilpreet applied and was accepted to Delhi University and successfully completed her Bachelor of Commerce Degree.

This wasn't the end of her educational pursuits, however. As she was approaching her last semesters at Delhi University, she had another discussion with her mother about going to the next level and pursuing her MBA. With her academic accomplishments, she again attained the support of her mother and father and applied to the Indian Institute of Planning and Management. For this degree, however, her parents made a shrewd deal with her and made their support for her MBA contingent upon Dilpreet agreeing to prioritize getting married and starting a family once she accomplished her MBA. As she looks back at her early years and her journey in overcoming the obstacles to her education and career goals, she saw that as she broke out of the mold of her family traditions, she had to be excellent at what she put her hands to in order to show that she was serious about what she wanted to accomplish. She needed to prove that she was worthy of the significant investment that was going to take place by her family. Breaking through these barriers was difficult and took time, but it was well worth it in the end. She sees that things are changing today in this area, but back then, for her, no one really understood why she was pursuing these goals. In her circumstances, she was pioneering something new within her family that has today become an example of success to her family and friends. As a result, her younger cousins are getting opportunities to get a good education, especially the girls!

True to her word, she met her future husband at the Indian Institute of Planning and Management. She completed her MBA in 2007 and joined the same global HR consulting firm that Puja joined in the same year. Together, with other team members, they would work to develop the new business research arm of that firm and develop a deep long-lasting friendship with one another. Puja and Dilpreet journeyed together for thirteen years, honing their skills and working with each area within the firm to provide insights that would be turned into market positioning white papers, go-to-market research for global and regional account planning, as well as research that would serve as a foundation to build business cases for opportunity deal pursuits. Over the years, they had strong contributions to the firm, and in 2019 and 2020, their team had built significant momentum and achieved a high level of credibility for their work. They were given high marks by their management team, and they believed that they had achieved a place of significance that would keep them safe from the rumors of layoffs in other areas of the firm due to the COVID pandemic. Downsizing activities were taking place in every market segment of the world.

A SIGNIFICANT SHIFT

On one typical day, Puja received a request at 5:30 p. m. India time to join a call with her manager in the US. This wasn't unusual because Puja was managing the team and thought that a new project had come up and there needed to be a discussion about it. Within minutes, she was told that due to market conditions, their entire research team was going to be laid off, that she would receive a certain amount of severance, and that she needed to pick her last day with the company. As the news spread throughout the team, Dilpreet and Puja spoke immediately and started processing what had just happened to them. It wasn't just the fact that they were suddenly losing their jobs, it was that they had built a significant bond of friendship over the years that was also being threatened by these unfortunate circumstances. On one hand, they knew that the firm was making significant changes to prepare itself for unknown market conditions, and on the other hand, they had put their heart and soul into their work, accomplishing their career goals and fueling their passion to provide world-class business research services. All of this stopped abruptly. The next day after they were let go, they met over the phone and concluded that they were not going to let these circumstances bog them down and shape their thinking for the future. This work was something that they had done for their entire career, and they decided to fight to continue to provide world-class business research to clients. Puja and Dilpreet discussed that they didn't want to work as employees at another company and take on the same risk of getting let go in those volatile markets. They decided on that very call to do their own business... a resilient restart! Their vision to start a company was born. What it would be called and what all the specific services would be was unclear to them, but they knew that they were going to restart their careers on their own. As they came together to plan next steps, Puja and Dilpreet brainstormed with a small group of people in the market that found value in what they were wanting to do. As they thought through scenarios, they felt that there was a need to help clients with search engine optimization. This would basically help clients get their valuable content to their target audience in a more effective way. As they went down that path, it became obvious to everyone that though this was a valid service, they needed to stay to their core capabilities and start creating relevant research reports that clients would buy. As this clicked with Puja and Dilpreet, the vision for Groundwork Intel began to emerge. Now they needed to figure out how to start a partnership company in India and begin to get their name out to let people know about their new venture. As they moved forward over the next month, they stayed singly focused on creating reports that they thought people would see as valuable and be willing to buy. They divided topics amongst themselves and, with all the passion and fire within themselves, created a repository of reports that they felt they could leverage to launch the company.

From being let go on April 25, 2020, to launching their new company website and announcing it to their LinkedIn network on June 5, 2020, they were on their way. How it would all work out, they didn't know. What they did know is that they were completely aligned in their passion and expertise, and they would take things one step at a time and do what they had always done: create world-class business insights. Through July and August of that year, they would have moments of getting some interest and encouragement, and when this happened, they were on the top of the world. There were other days when things were slow, and they had frustrations and thoughts of great discouragement. The ups and downs were tough as they had great expectations with little traction in the marketplace. Even though it was tough, they were determined to stay the course and believe that they were going to win in the end. Their friendship became their strength as they encouraged each other on the good days and on the hard days. Both Puja and Dilpreet said that, alone, they might not have stayed the course. Together, however, they were a force and they knew it. They respected each other and they trusted each other. They were honest with each other. When one was struggling, each person looked to the strengths of the other person and it pulled them through. They divide their responsibilities based on their strengths, not their egos. If it needs to be done, they divide and conquer. When they make mistakes, they find a way to laugh about it, because they know that they are doing their best in forging a new path for themselves. There is a humility that they share that allows them to draw from each other. They both see the teamwork in what they are doing. Neither one of them takes credit for themselves and this has been part of their friendship for the last fifteen years. They have a shared vision and a dream to build something together. This bond, with focus and determination, drives their pursuit to excellence in everything that they do. As they focus on building each other up, as their platform expands, they are building a healthy safe company culture of authentic teaming. Many people talk about it, but for Puja and Dilpreet, it comes from within and it's natural to them.

BREAKTHROUGH MOMENTS

July, August, and September of 2020 were tough months. Puja and Dilpreet were having lots of conversations and doing quite a bit of pro bono work with potential clients hoping to generate business, but nothing was coming their way regarding revenue. They were finding interest, but key sponsorship and funding for projects became a problem. They stuck to their plan, and at the end of September, everything changed. It was a small change, but a significant one. They received their first contract to provide monthly business research services to a local client. For Dilpreet, this was her breakthrough moment for the business. She knew inside of herself that the company was going to grow from there.

Shortly after this victory, they brought in another local client but on a three-month trial. There were concerns with this client that Puja and Dilpreet were a start-up and didn't know if they were worth the risk in giving them a long-term contract. Because of all the layoffs that were happening, they needed to prove to this client that Groundwork Intel was something that they were going to build and grow. After the three-month trial, they more than demonstrated their capabilities along with their passion to grow their company.

With two clients coming in one after another, this was Puja's breakthrough moment where she knew that it was only going to go up from here. In a market when companies were pulling back spending during the pandemic, they needed to stay focused and keep encouraging people to try them. Even after the two engagements were in place, they continued doing pro bono and pilot work to demonstrate their capabilities. It was just the two of them, and at times, prospective companies were concerned that they didn't have the bandwidth to survive. They stayed the course and kept assuring people that they were in this for good. New business was sporadic through the rest of the year, but in January of 2021, opportunities began to build again. The firm that they separated from reached out for support, which was a huge compliment to them and it continued to validate their company model and represented a third stable client!Building out their team became a critical part of their journey at this time. They had been working very well together, as they had for years. With bandwidth constraints coming up, they brainstormed about how they could grow their team. Between the two of them, they had developed a company culture of excellence, humility, trust, and safety. Now they needed to build this out and bring others in that could share their vision while maintaining excellent service to their clients. With all the people that had been laid off in India, they knew that there were many highly educated and intelligent women that had been displaced. The question that they had was how to find the right people, and in short order. As they came together to plan, they decided first off that they wanted to build an all-woman team—women that were facing some of the same challenges in the marketplace that they had faced, as well as challenges that were beyond what their personal experiences were like. They explained that in India, in a typical situation, the husband's career is the primary career. As a result, if a woman had a large tier one city job before they got married, as soon as they got married, if he was in a medium tier two size city or a small tier three size city, she would move to accommodate his career. This phenomenon created a highly skilled, highly educated workforce in tier 2 and 3 cities that they could potentially tap into. Now with the COVID impact upon them, a 2021 report from the Center for Sustainable Employment at Azim Premji University in India showed that during the first lockdown in 2020, only 7 percent of men lost their jobs, compared to 47 percent of women who lost their jobs and did not return to work by the end of the year.

According to the same report, Indian women also spent more time doing unpaid care work at home than men. On average, they spent 9.8 times more time than men on unpaid domestic chores and 4.5 hours a day caring for children, elders, and the sick. During the pandemic, their share of unpaid care work grew by nearly 30 percent.

According to *The New Indian Press*, in an article called, "Tackling the Shadow Pandemic of Rising Domestic Violence" on October 19, 2020, India recorded a 2.5 time increase in domestic violence between February and May of 2020. Some women's organizations reported that in the first four phases of the lockdown, they received more reports of domestic violence than they had in the last ten years for a similar period of time. Others indicated that many women were unable to report the violence, as they had less privacy and means to access help.

Based on these facts, with great passion and conviction, they decided to focus on: giving qualified women opportunities who had lost their jobs; providing highly educated women a tier 1 city career experience when they lived in a tier 2 or tier 3 city; and lastly, providing a flexible work schedule to accommodate supporting a family and focusing on project deliverables, not punching a clock at an office. They knew that if they could find women in this situation, they would secure the talent that they were looking for to grow their company. They also knew that their plan would create an unending pipeline of talent as their business needs diversified and grew. With a solid plan to move forward, they started networking with friends, former colleagues, and business contacts to build out a solid pipeline of candidates. As they readied themselves to grow, they were able to start thinking about balancing the delivery responsibilities with the potential new team members so that they could focus on business development, doing quality reviews on project deliverables, and taking care of some of the administrative things that come with an expanding business. Preparing to grow their team couldn't have come at a better time. Soon after their third client signed on, international projects started to develop in their pipeline. They were well versed in this type of work and were working hard to get the chance to break into their forte. With focus and hard work, in February and March of 2021, two additional clients—one headquartered in Switzerland and one headquartered in the US—were signed! They closed three international projects between the two clients, and they were now operating in Asia, Europe, and the US. At this point in time, they were providing business research and talent mapping services to key HR consulting and executive search firms.

As they continued to work with clients and gain momentum, they realized two very tangible dynamics taking place in the market that came into their favor. First, they knew based on their experience that there was a need. As the COVID phenomenon increased, however, they didn't realize that it would exponentially impact the need for businesses to have more accurate and timely insights into the market, their clients, and their competitors.

Second, they realized that they were also building momentum in the marketplace by expanding their team. With every new loyal team member, they were gaining access to key contacts and leads that added to the momentum of expanding their business.

With these two dynamics working together for them, 2021 started off being a great year. At their one-year anniversary in June of 2021, these two founders had established a profitable start-up in India leveraging an agile Gig business model. Their team had grown from two to eight! They served seventeen clients where 75 percent of them represented repeat business. Two of their clients were in the top 10 global executive search firms and they also supported boutique advisory companies, management consulting firms, market research organizations, financial services, and consumer goods companies. By the end of this first year, 45 percent of their revenue was coming from the US and Europe. By any standards, their resilient restart was established in the market and the only direction that they would go is up!As we fast forward to February 2023, they have a total of 40+ key clients across the globe and their offerings have grown to encompass both talent intelligence and business research. Services in these areas include:

Talent Intelligence: human capital trends, organization structure and operating model benchmarking, talent mapping, HR transformation case studies, rewards benchmarking, white papers/perspectives on HR topics, etc.

Business Research: company diagnostics, competitor and market intelligence, sector insights, thematic research, hypothesis validation, social media content creation, etc.

They started with 30 years of combined experience, a vision for a resilient restart, and a love and passion to provide information in a way that will help business leaders make the best decisions possible in turbulent times. Now that they have seen with their own eyes the accomplishments that they have made, their vision has grown to expand their team to 50 within three years. Puja and Dilpreet have gotten the attention of senior leaders in India that are willing to stand by them, mentor them, and help them win. One such person is Mr. Rajiv Krishnan, an accomplished leader in the human capital advisory space, who has provided invaluable advice and insight. In addition to this, they have received three tangible offers from reputable companies to acquire them. Most importantly, though, they have the emotional and financial support of their husbands. While Puja was employed, her entrepreneurial husband, Vishal Vij, was regularly planting seeds within her that she should go out on her own someday. When they decided to start Groundwork Intel, he was a pillar of strength and continually encourages her and motivates her every step of the way. For Dilpreet, her husband, Humjeet Singh, has always been supportive of her career, whether it was getting a job after the completion of her MBA or after she gave birth to their child. When she was informed that she was losing her corporate job, he let her know that she would succeed in the next chapter of her work and he enthusiastically supports her with Groundwork Intel. Both husbands celebrate every client win and stand firmly behind what Puja and Dilpreet are accomplishing. All of this provides a confirmation to them that they are on the right track and that they have more to do on their own. They are just getting started!

ENTREPRENEURIAL INSIGHTS

As I reflect on their journey, I think about several key things that have made Puja and Dilpreet's resilient restart a success.

THEY OVERCAME WHEN THEY WERE YOUNG (5-OVERCOME)

When I look at the hardships that Puja and her family went through when her father died suddenly, and the lifestyle that they had to take on in order to rise above it, you can see that it shaped her into the person that she is today. At a young age, Puja made a decision that she would overcome difficult circumstances. The example of her mother to push through paved a way for Puja to do the same. When you look at the hardships that Dilpreet went through—having a dream to have a career and to become highly educated when no one in her family was doing that or initially saw the significance of it—never giving up on her dream shaped her. Over her entire childhood, she needed to provide tangible examples of being responsible, doing well in school, and honoring her present condition. The hardships that you overcome become your strengths. The hardships that defeat you hold you back. When Puja and Dilpreet decided to start Groundwork Intel, they showed up with the strengths that shaped them when they were young.

PASSION TO PROVIDE ACCURATE AND TIMELY INFORMATION TO BUSINESS LEADERS (6-EXCELLENCE)

They actually know themselves really well. They are honest with themselves and with each other to the point that they are able to laugh at their mistakes and then make better decisions the next time around. They know each other's strengths and weaknesses and it only makes them better as a partnership. Knowing that they both individually and collectively want to contribute to the foundation of building business insights for leaders is incredible. Being excellent in their work as a team gave them one option when they decided to start their own business: "We will do this ONE thing well: provide valuable insights to leaders."

RESOLUTE DECISION TO GO ON THEIR OWN (7-RESOLVE)

Everyone has defining moments when hardships are thrust upon them. There are people that walk around and talk about how unfair life is, and then there are people that use their creativity, gifts, and passions to address hardships and push through them. Puja and Dilpreet represent the latter. When they were let go, they were hurt, frustrated, and knocked off of their proverbial horse. Their reaction was amazing. "We're going to start our own company!" Amazingly, a couple of days after they were let go, on the same day, at the same time, they both came to that conclusion. Once they set their eyes on starting their own company, they never looked back; they only looked ahead.

UNWAVERING FOCUS ON THEIR VISION IN UNCERTAIN TIMES (8-FOCUS)

Having a single focus and vision is one thing. Sticking to it in uncertain times is quite another. The time frame for each individual moving out into something new and facing uncertain times varies by individual. What seems to define the success of uncertain times for everyone is the position of the heart to persevere. If there is a crack in that foundation, a deep hidden doubt, or an insecurity that nags at you, it will definitely slow you down or even stop you from attaining your goals. The goal isn't to be void of issues; it's to confront the issues with honesty and transparency. Puja and Dilpreet said that they depended on each other to be strong when the other was weak. We know that they are both strong in humility. By being true honest friends with each other, they were able to weather the storm in uncertain times. They said, "Alone, we probably would have quit." Together, they became unstoppable!

A HEART TO SERVE OTHERS (3-GIVER)

In a world where it is easy to let others know how much you care, the opportunity to remind everyone that you are a giving person is all around us. Don't get me wrong, I love hearing stories on social media of someone being at the right place at the right time to make a difference. I find, however, that leaders that live a lifestyle of sacrificial giving rarely, if ever, talk about it themselves. I see this quality in Puja and Dilpreet. Building a company that supports the well-being of women in their country and then making it a key part of who they are in the marketplace is impressive. It isn't that they are anti-men; it's that they are addressing a need and an imbalance in their current society. I know that they are selflessly invested in their team and in each other, and it's infectious.

TRANSPARENT LEADERSHIP BASED ON THE POWER OF HUMILITY (9-HUMILITY)

Have you ever met someone that, as soon as you shake their hand or hear them speak, you know that they are coming from a powerful place of humility and strength and you immediately respect them? When I first met Puja and Dilpreet, I felt that. As I heard them tell their story and why they do the things that they do, I could tell it comes from a deep sense of purpose within them. When they stay up all night to make sure that their deliverables are world-class or when they put a team member first before themselves, it represents the glue that holds them together and sets them up for a very bright future.

CHAPTER THREE

GAME-CHANGING INNOVATION

The Chris Borroni-Bird Story

THE VISIONS, IDEAS, and technologies that work together to make the movement of things more powerful, efficient, sustainable, cheaper, and safer has never been more robust across each sector of the marketplace. Across the gamut of new energy solutions, software, firmware, communications, artificial intelligence, and common and uncommon corporate alliances, there is a feverish drive to bring breakthrough innovation to all things mobility. For the winners of this race, the upside financial impact will be astronomical. For the losers, it will be business as usual, and then a slow fade out of prominence.

There are leaders in the world of game-changing innovation that realize that even though drones, jet packs, hoverboards, space travel, and autonomous technologies are important to the future of transportation, there are many people in the world that require much less sophistication in order to make their world a better place. Bringing a simple mobility device to the poorest of the poor to help them haul water and materials in a more efficient way can transform their existence. Chris Borroni-Bird, a Cambridge PhD graduate and significant contributor to advanced mobility solutions in the automotive and communications industries for three decades, is one of those leaders. While doing some relief work in Mali, he felt a deep tug in his heart for the people of Sub-Saharan Africa and eventually India. He saw that bringing a simple mobility solution to this people group would profoundly impact their lives. Chris founded Afreecar in 2018 to bring his vision to life. His story will inspire the game-changing innovator in you.

HISTORY AND BACKGROUND

Chris was born in 1964 and grew up in Liverpool, England. His parents are from Brighton and Hong Kong and Chris is the youngest of four kids. He grew up in a working-class family in a very small home, less than one thousand square feet with one bathroom. It was a very simple upbringing by today's standards, but it was all that he knew. At the age of sixteen in 1983, Chris graduated from St. John Rigby College. With Chris' academic accomplishments, he was offered admission into King's College at Cambridge University. At that time, he was the first person from St. John Rigby to attend Cambridge. When Chris arrived there, his world exploded as he was instantly exposed to people from all over the country—and all over the world. With an insatiable desire to learn, he placed his focus on science and technology. Chris successfully soared through his Bachelor's degree at Cambridge in the department of Natural Sciences, which included the study of physics, chemistry, mathematics, materials, and biology. Chris' focus area was in chemistry. Toward the conclusion of his Bachelor's degree, Cambridge approached him and asked him to pursue his PhD there. Chris was very excited, but he was interested in studying under Sir David Anthony King, Brunner Professor of Physical Chemistry at the University of Liverpool, who was recognized as the leader in his field in England and around the world. Chris was able to schedule a meeting with him to discuss his academic aspirations. After Chris met with him, he was certain that he wanted to be taught and mentored by King. It was a difficult decision for Chris to consider leaving Cambridge and do his PhD at another university. Despite the advice from his family and friends to stay at Cambridge, he made a very calculating decision to follow King to the University of Liverpool.

Chris made an excellent choice to align with King, as he would become very influential in England and became a key part of several prestigious universities, while also becoming the Chief Science Advisor for former Prime Minister Tony Blair. He had great impact during that time in dealing with Mad Cow Disease and became world renowned in crafting key insights and policies around global warming. Chris was in Liverpool for about a year when an amazing thing happened. King was offered, and accepted, the prestigious 1920 Chair of Physical Chemistry at Cambridge. Chris was elated, packed his bags, and moved back to Cambridge to complete his PhD under King. As excited as Chris was to continue his education, the biggest challenge of his academic studies was about to unfold. King challenged Chris to take a leap into the unknown. He challenged him to go deep into researching the heat release measurement and catalytic capability of specific nanometer-thick metal films. Within the automotive and petrochemical industries, there still wasn't a reliable process to test these catalytic materials with any predictability. This uncertainty added to the research and development costs in bringing new products to the market. With Chris' project, he was going to create the process to measure the materials, and also create the machine that could quantify the results in a systematic way. The title of his research project was called, Single Crystal Absorption Microcalorimetry.

Chris had a slow start and it was a nerve-wracking experience. He could see other students in the lab steadily working through their PhD initiatives, as many of them were leveraging machines that had already been built. As a result, they were conducting experiments in a very stable environment. Because Chris was inventing his machine, he had to move at a slower pace. With all that he was managing, it forced him to realize the possibility that he wasn't going to graduate on time if he couldn't get the machine built and operational.

Chris spent many sleepless nights pouring over his work and eventually he was able to invent the testing machine. From there, he had to debug it, enhance it, and all the while design the experiments that would yield a clear and concise groundbreaking result. One amazing November day in 1990, he got the result that he needed. With an enormous amount of elation, he saw that he was going to complete his project on time! He wrote his results up over the course of a few months and received his PhD with his class. As Chris reflected back on his PhD journey, he saw that King's challenge was rooted in the fact that he saw an untapped potential in Chris that needed to be drawn out. Overcoming the challenge gave Chris a newfound confidence in himself and showed him that he could take something that no one had ever done and bring it to life. Now that all of the pressure of the program had come off of him, he began planning his future. Soon after Chris graduated, he married Laura Borroni and they moved to Japan where he did some post-doctoral work at the University of Tokyo. Chris was going back and forth on whether or not he was going to pursue an academic career or move into the marketplace. During his time in Tokyo, he made a significant decision to pursue opportunities within the automotive industry. He began applying for jobs in England and in the United States.

MARKETPLACE DEVELOPMENTS

Not long after he started sending his resume out to prospective companies, a relationship developed between Chris and senior leaders of the Research and Development team at Chrysler. Chrysler was going through a lot of pain in the marketplace in the late 1980s and early 1990s and they were focused intensely on turning things around. As a result of the difficult times, one of the things that Chrysler did was to institute a hiring freeze. It seemed bleak that Chris would join Chrysler due to those conditions, not to mention that he also required a work visa. As Chris continued his discussions with Chrysler, he felt that he could make a significant impact at the company and he hoped that he could start his marketplace contribution there. Chris had key sponsors that built a case for him to join. Eventually he received an exception to the hiring freeze and was approved by Chrysler's senior leadership. Chris started at Chrysler in 1992. Now that the

Cold War threat was over, there was a whole host of protected technology that was housed within the National Labs that was being shared with corporations in order to improve American competitiveness. Chris, with a keen ability to understand the material in the National Labs, was initially tasked with helping Chrysler leverage this technology in order to improve its position in the marketplace. As Chrysler began developing future vehicle mobility concepts, Chris helped them focus on fuel cell technology as a key approach. As a result, Chris became their key fuel cell specialist. Chris was able to see beyond the fuel cell as a standalone technology and started seeing the power of integrating technology and design as a game-changing concept. He eventually became the fuel cell vehicle manager and took responsibility for the entire vehicle. This role opened doors to Chris and he began building momentum in exploring the art of the possible for future mobility. As the 1990s progressed, change was in the air for Chrysler, and on May 7, 1998, Daimler-Benz purchased Chrysler for $36 billion. This was an unprecedented event in the automobile industry, and in the country, as it was the largest corporate purchase of a US company by a foreign buyer. With Daimler taking over Chrysler, Chris felt that a shift was taking place in philosophy as it related to how technology was viewed and how it would be integrated into the design of the vehicle. Two years after the acquisition, Chris decided to think about joining another team. Discussions started taking place with General Motors and Chris saw that they were in lockstep with their mutual desires to create a future mobility concept from the ground up. In June of 2000, Chris joined General Motors and created a new Design and Technology Fusion group. With senior leader sponsorship, Chris' first assignment was to think about how to create a vehicle design around fuel cell technology. At that same time, Chris saw the emergence of chassis-by-wire technologies and how this could reinvent the interior by eliminating pedals and steering wheels, which also has a significant impact on autonomous driving implementations. The fuel cell, like a battery, eliminates the engine compartment and creates a flat floor, giving designers exterior styling freedom to go along with interior design freedom. By combining fuel cell and chassis-by-wire technologies, and leveraging the design possibilities of both, Chris was able to create the autonomy concept and the "skateboard" chassis was born. The significance of the autonomy chassis skateboard is that it offers electric vehicles the ability to streamline the electronics, driving features, motors, and associated energy components within one chassis concept. This approach allows car manufacturers the ability to reduce the complexity and associated costs of research and development for their electric vehicle platforms (Reference: The Next Avenue Article, May 27, 2020). As Chris looked back on his career at this point in time, he saw that starting as a fuel cell specialist, moving to a fuel cell vehicle manager, and overseeing vehicle design gave him a rich perspective on what was possible. By leading these areas, he was able to open up the palette of creativity for the future. He was also seeing the significant societal impacts of using fuel cell technology by addressing the five constraints of urban mobility: 1) pollution, 2) energy consumption, 3) accidents, 4) congestion, and 5) urban parking. By leveraging technology to design vehicles around societal needs, Chris' vision became more complete and he saw clearly how this approach could have a significant impact on aligning the future of mobility with serving the overall needs of people and the planet. These mobility approaches were ahead of their time in the industry and continue to be developed in the market today. Though many of the patents that Chris and his team produced have expired, other automakers, like Tesla, continue to take the autonomy chassis skateboard concept to the next levels of innovation by bridging the gaps between the traditional automobile and technology.

GAME-CHANGING MOMENT

While still at General Motors in 2008, Chris had a game-changing moment as he was doing some relief work in Mali, Sub-Sahara Africa, with some friends. Chris noticed two patterns of activity in the village that fascinated him. He first noticed that there was a person in the village, an entrepreneur, that was renting batteries to people. After they were depleted, the people would bring them back and the entrepreneur would charge them during the day, using a solar panel, and rent them out again. As there isn't gasoline or wind power to speak of, solar power in the Sub-Sahara is king.

The second thing he saw was all the activity around walking. He saw that they were walking miles to haul water for daily use and to conduct trade with other villages. As an expert innovator in his field, Chris concluded that if a mobility solution could be created by leveraging solar power to reduce walking time and reduce the effort to haul goods, people could spend more time with their families, create extra time to enhance their trade, and potentially free up time for education. Chris then researched the potential societal impacts of a solution for off-grid mobility and saw that over one billion people could be impacted across Sub-Saharan Africa and India. This need was too much for him to disregard. He knew that, in large part, most of the materials for a solution were already invented. He just needed to assemble a solution that was inexpensive, easy to use, durable, and powered by solar in order to bring a mobility solution to life. After Chris' experiences in Mali, he was never the same. Over time, this became his endgame career goal. He felt that if he could apply his capabilities to the automotive industry until it was time to retire, he could then throw everything at his mobility solution for Africa and India. He called this initiative Afreecar.

MARKETPLACE DEVELOPMENTS CONTINUED

In August of 2012, Chris left GM to expand his expertise. He became a vice president of research and development at Qualcomm to help influence their groundbreaking vehicle to pedestrian (V2P) communications and wireless EV charging. Qualcomm's automotive business, at that time, was supplying modems to a top automotive company. Qualcomm's goal was to repurpose existing technology into the automotive sector. The majority of their research and development was focused on the smartphone and the automotive sector was considered to be too small of a market to justify its own R&D focus. During Chris' five years at the company, he helped shift the mindset around the future of the automotive market by showing that one of the most significant future phases of technology will be to leverage the automobile as a future technology compute platform. Today, if your smartphone stops working, it's inconvenient, but it won't keep you from getting to your destination. Consider the computing power and versatility requirements for autonomous driving and what they need to achieve in order to accommodate vibration, extreme hot and cold, resilience against cyberattack, and have software and hardware redundancy for reliability in case of a failure. The winner of this race, by pulling all of these elements together, will have a significant impact on the future of computing across not only the automotive market, but others like the military and healthcare markets, as well.

Qualcomm, Intel, Nvidia, Huawei, and others are in a race now and it will be interesting to see who will come in first place.

Chris left Qualcomm in 2017 and spent a brief time as a research scientist at the Massachusetts Institute of Technology (MIT) and then at Waymo as chief engineer for future vehicles. His focus was to develop requirements for a ground-up robotaxi. During this time, however, Afreecar continued to be in the forefront of his mind. After much contemplation, he knew that it was time for him to step down from Waymo and dedicate himself fully to the Afreecar project.

AFREECAR COMES TO LIFE

In 2018, Afreecar was born and it was time for Chris to bring his mobility solution to life in order to serve the poorest of poor. The first use case was put together with the support of Pratt & Miller Engineering, a groundbreaking product development company. The team created a small solar powered trailer that was attached to a bicycle. The idea behind it was that the bicycle could operate by itself, but when the trailer was attached, it could provide power assist to the bicycle as needed. The trailer could then sit and charge at its destination while the bicycle could go off and do other things. In a two-person scenario, for example, the trailer could be set up in a market to sell goods with one person, all the while charging while it sits. The person on the bicycle could deliver goods door to door so that you can provide two marketplace functions at the same time. Even though the initial concept was sound, Chris was challenged with the fact that these types of small trailers are not typical in Africa. What they have is more like a wheelbarrow that has a flat top for hauling things. As Chris was working on which two-, three-, or four-wheeled vehicles to add mobility to, he felt that picking just one wasn't going to work, as there were too many to consider. He then concluded that it wouldn't be possible to pick one standard. It became clear to him that he needed to create a solution that could be applied to almost any vehicle that could be pushed, pulled, or pedaled. As he developed his idea, it became apparent to him that this mobility device could also be applied to hospital beds, wheelchairs, gurneys, and wheel carts. He saw that if he could offer a briefcase-sized kit to help provide mobility to developing economies to improve their life, it could also be applied to solutions in the developed world to apply aid where it's needed. As he further expanded his thinking, he saw that this device could also be a source of power to electric water pumps, cell phones, and ventilators. This became a significant transformation of his idea that took a specific point solution from a small trailer to a transferable small device to power a variety of small vehicles with an e-kit that would offer a reasonable low price point. This also increased the applicability to each individual, because if a person knows how to operate their handcart, for example, all they need to do is add the power assist and then the burden of pushing, pulling, or pedaling could be taken care of by the device. In contrast, an all-electric hand cart is very expensive, where adding power assist via Chris' concept will allow you to add a mobility solution at a very affordable cost, and it can be manufactured in a country like Africa or India, where the labor and material costs are lower. Chris began to realize that the e-kit could transform lives in multi-dimensional ways. As Chris continues to travel around the world, he can see that this can easily become the work to which he dedicates his life. He sees that bringing affordable and sustainable mobility to the world, which will enhance the economic development of many people groups, is going to be a lifelong journey for him. Chris' vision is to diversify the manufacturing of the e-kit to local and regional companies to enhance the economic development of each area. He believes that this will further improve the local economy and bring the solution to a more local level. Chris sees it is often simple solutions that can easily solve very complex problems. For example, an electric vehicle today has something like a one-hundred-kilowatt engine and a one-hundred-kilowatt hour battery. Chris' e-kit might have a one-kilowatt motor, a little more than one horsepower, and a one-kilowatt hour battery. His e-kit is one hundred times less powerful, but it can provide a solution that can improve the lives of over one billion people. Chris sees endless potential impact for his solution. The e-kit will also bring a form of independence from oil companies, electric utilities, and central governments. Individuals and communities can also become self-sufficient to create the e-kit by harvesting existing and recycled materials.

This vision, which is becoming a reality, will allow Chris to dedicate his life to helping the people in Sub-Saharan Africa and India that are in great need for a mobility solution. This is something that is first and foremost in his heart.

FUNDING STRATEGY

With any start-up, funding can be difficult. Chris has also found this to be true. He has self-funded certain parts of his research, received support from local corporations, and has received support from local universities. This has slowed the process down, but it has only strengthened his resolve to keep moving. As Chris continues to leverage his experience from his automotive career, he finds that he is able to network with companies that are focused on leveraging electric vehicles. He is working with an Indian company that is working to leverage electric vehicles for commercial goods delivery. As a result, they are interested in building low speed electric vehicles based on the autonomy chassis skateboard concept. As they consulted with Chris, it gave him the opportunity to tell his Afreecar story and see if they could leverage each other moving forward. This particular Indian company wants to work in a specific market, but it won't compete with the market that Chris wants to address. This company, and others like it, might be a great solution for Chris as they can help each other without channel conflict. They can leverage insights, perspectives, low-cost manufacturing and assembly, materials, and associated supply chains to benefit each other. Chris has also received support from the state of Michigan, the Michigan Economic Development Corporation (MEDC), Oakland University, and the Toyota Mobility Foundation. Chris has just begun a new leg of his journey! The more that people from all walks of life become aware of the issue that he is working to address, the more support he is receiving. He recently received the SAE Create the Future award and he is being asked to speak on Afreecar and the future of mobility with top organizations like the Automotive Hall of Fame, where top automotive educators gather from the nations' top design schools. Based on Chris' focus on game-changing innovation, there is no doubt that he will attain the results that he is looking for!

ENTREPRENEURIAL INSIGHTS

Having spent time with Chris to understand his career journey and his passion to bring game-changing innovation to the poorest of the poor, I see several entrepreneurial impacts.

HE SIGNS UP TO CONQUER THE BIG UNKNOWNS (10-FEARLESS)

Chris has demonstrated a pattern throughout his life of signing up to conquer some really big unknowns. From 1) being the first person from St. John Rigby College to go to Cambridge; to 2) agreeing to a PhD topic that had never been done before; 3) jumping into the automotive industry to lead in the technology, design, and societal impacts of future mobility; to 4) becoming the founder of a mobility company that serves the poorest of the poor. There is a resolute strength, a quiet calm, and a fearlessness that propels Chris into adventure.

A FOCUS ON INDIVIDUALS (11-SEE)

There are a lot of influences in the global marketplace. What

I notice about Chris is that he sees people through all of the different agendas that are out there. For example, it is often the case that the university that you attend can influence what choices you make. Their brand can offer certain opportunities in the marketplace that may not come with other university affiliations. Chris chose to pursue a relationship with Sir David Anthony King, and leave Cambridge to do it. And when King was invited to come to Cambridge, Chris returned and graduated from there. When Chris entered into the marketplace, he again chose to align himself with key members of Chrysler's R&D team. He saw how these leaders relentlessly sponsored him and gave him his start in the automotive industry. Chris significantly valued his relationship with Tom Moore (Chrysler's research leader) throughout his career. As Chris started working with key members of R&D at General Motors, he was able to bring the elements of technology, design, and societal impacts all together under one leadership team. He was then able to demonstrate the capabilities of GM by helping to create a 20-year vision for the future of mobility at the 2010 Shanghai World Expo. As Chris started dreaming about Afreecar, he was able to take all of his education and experience and step up to be the individual to follow as he serves the low-income people of Africa and India. Chris has consistently focused on key people to follow and now he is focusing on people that he can serve.

NOT THE BIGGEST VOICE IN THE ROOM (12-LISTEN)

When I met Chris for the first time, he was working at General Motors. What stood out to me was that he wasn't the biggest voice in the room. He is a quiet profound listener. He appreciates discussion and debate, but never with a desire to convince or push, but to understand. He wants to find the best approach to solving problems. I see that he hungers for perspective and looks for every way to bring it out of whomever he is spending time with. After gathering multiple facets of understanding, by listening to the many voices in the room, he moves out with a strategic approach that has tremendous long-lasting impact.

WILLING TO LAY IT ALL ON THE LINE (13-SACRIFICE)

I have the privilege of meeting and spending time with some of the most respected movers and shakers in the industrial sector. Chris is absolutely one of those people. As being one of the leading mobility innovators of our time, he is determined to see his vision through. He doesn't have two or three core pursuits, he has one: to help the poorest of the poor. For this core pursuit, he uses all of his gifts, talents, network, education, and experience to lay it all on the line to see Afreecar expand and grow. He knows that it will take time and stretch him beyond his imagination. He doesn't do it for a monument in his name; he does it because he sees the needs of people and wants to make their lives better. When Afreecar succeeds, people will win, and this will be Chris' greatest reward.

CHAPTER FOUR

CREATIVE INGENUITY

The Sarah Schneider Story

GETTING INTO THE restaurant business is not for the faint at heart. Most independent restaurants don't make it to their fourth-year anniversary. There are many reasons why this is the case. With steep competition, rising payroll, and food costs, it's easy for things to get out of control. Adding the COVID factor into the mix makes things that much more difficult, if not impossible, to achieve your original vision of success. It takes someone with creative ingenuity to survive, someone with a heart to serve people and bring amazing food every time someone sits at one of their tables. It's fusing business acumen, crazy creativity, and a hunger to do it better each and every day. Sarah Schneider is a person that demonstrates this type of creative ingenuity day in and day out. Sarah always enjoyed creating unique and special dining moments for her family and friends. Over time, a dream developed in her heart to bring a fresh and new dining experience to her community in downtown Clarkston, Michigan. With the tremendous backing of her husband James, her dream became a reality and The Fed Community was born. As a first-time restaurant owner, and sometimes against all odds, Sarah led the transformation of a historic bank building into a place for the community to gather, which has now become a destination for people from around the state, the US, and the world.

BACKGROUND AND HISTORY

Sarah Carmichael was born in Redford, Michigan, just outside of Detroit. When she was in the third grade, her family moved to Waterford, Michigan, where she grew up. Her father graduated from the University of Michigan with an engineering degree but never went to work as an engineer; instead, he made his living as a very talented artist in clay sculpture and then later on established himself in steel art. Her mother, a nurse and also an artist, focused her creativity on basket weaving, creating rugs and sweaters, and also developed a porcelain jewelry line.

Being surrounded by artistic energy, and the fact that her father's studio was in their home, Sarah was encouraged and enabled to express herself through her art. Having open access to his studio gave her a regular opportunity to paint, play with clay, and dabble with his tools, materials, and equipment. When she was in grade school, she made soap dishes in clay, painted them, fired them, and then put them in her wagon and sold them for ten cents apiece.

She would imagine having a store and then set up whatever came to her mind, whether it was a grocery store, an art gallery, or a clothing store. She was free to dream and create based on her very active imagination. If she could see it, she could bring it to life. Her ideas came and they never seemed to stop. She was creating all of the time. As she got older, she started incorporating design concepts into her ideas. Any money that she made babysitting, she would pour into redecorating her bedroom. She would change the furniture around and paint the walls. When she was tired of the seafoam green carpet in her bedroom, she decided to hire a carpet dyer while her parents were away at an art show in order to change it to gray.

The great part about Sarah was that she was an active dreamer with the ability to create what she saw in her mind's eye. As she entered into high school, however, she found that not everyone appreciated her creative passion. She felt that many of her teachers couldn't relate to her, and at times, she had a difficult time relating to them. She was being put in circumstances where she felt that she was being constrained, and they told her that she lacked focus and initiative. There were a few teachers that really got where Sarah was coming from and they were a breath of fresh air to her, and that fueled her ingenuity. She learned a lot about herself in high school and came to the realization that she has a creative brain, and along with that, a drive to see her creations come to life. She saw that she may not be able to excel in every environment, but that she could definitely excel when she has the freedom to dream and to create. With high school being difficult for her, she also struggled as she began her college studies. Her parents, wanting her to get her college education, challenged her to do well in community college before they sent her off to a university. Unfortunately, she continued to have a hard time excelling at school with the constraints of a traditional learning environment. Before long, she abandoned her efforts to finish college and started thinking about what was next for her.

When she added it all up in her mind, Sarah felt that she needed to be in a place where she could flow creatively and not be constrained. Sarah made a bold plan to move to New York to be part of the arts and entertainment business with a desire to become an actor. In 1996, she made the move but found it impossible to get into an apartment. She joined a close friend that was living there just for the summer months. They knew that they needed to find a long-term place if her plan was going to work. Together they stood in line after line applying for apartments, but everything came up empty for them. Out of time to find a permanent place, they returned to Michigan after the summer and started immediately thinking about what was next. One key thing they realized was that teaming up to combine their resources was the best way forward. As they gathered their thoughts, they came to the conclusion that they would target Los Angeles instead of going back to New York. Their plan was the same: to get engrained in the arts and entertainment industry and see what opportunities might open for acting. While still in Michigan, they decided to work as much as they could before heading out to California. They were both able to save about nine hundred dollars apiece. They heard of successful actors that started out with meager beginnings and hoped that things would open for them, too. They packed their cars to capacity and made their way west. They arrived in LA and it didn't take them long to find an apartment. Things were starting out well and they were excited about their new beginning. It wasn't an easy road. They lived paycheck to paycheck and took every opportunity to work. They would stand in lines to be extras in shows and movies and make $40 at a time. It wasn't much, but they were excited that they were getting active in the world that they longed to be part of. Not too long after being there, Sarah was able to get her Screen

Actors Guild (SAG) card. Being part of the actors' union provided a little more money for her efforts, but it was still tough. Eventually, Sarah and her friend joined the Auto Show circuit as speakers and narrators. They could have their home base in LA, travel with the Auto Show, and then when they returned to LA, they worked as much as they could in the entertainment industry. They took advantage of every open door and attended movie premiers, private entertainment events, and intimate dinner parties. They were making it work and getting a chance to see how the industry operated from the inside out. At one dinner party in particular, the host hired a private chef and decorated the home in a very special way. The atmosphere seemed electric and it really struck a heart chord deep within Sarah. She felt so special at the event. It resonated so well with her personality that she made a decision at that very moment to host parties like this in her future. She had no extra money and no idea how she would pull this vision off, but she knew that it was going to be in her future, just as she knew that she could succeed in LA. Even though her present situation showed that she was barely making it financially, her dreams kept her future prospects alive and also allowed her to continue to hope for her breakthrough moments. Sarah had always appreciated the fusion between art, decorating, and creating an atmosphere to bring about special moments. After this experience, however, she became acutely aware of the design ideas at every hotel, restaurant, and event location that she participated in. It was something that she was storing inside herself for the future. Sarah was building momentum and getting great opportunities to act and also to be part of special events. For example, she was an assistant to the producer for a New Year's Eve event featuring a world-renowned singer and actor. She worked every day with an illustrious composer that provided the music for the event. Sarah got a front row seat on how amazing and talented people worked together to put on a world-class event. Sarah could see a bright future for herself in LA, but at the same time, she was also longing for something else: a family of her own. She started to wonder if LA was the place where she could make both of these desires work together.

COURSE CHANGE

After four years of being in LA, one day she woke up and concluded that for her, LA wasn't the place to meet someone and raise a family. As much as she loved the city, she didn't believe that she could make that happen there. It was hard for her to consider letting go of her dream, but while she was there, she grew tremendously as a person. She had the opportunity to learn, not in a formal class room, but through her experiences of dreaming, taking risks, and then being accountable to make it work out. It wasn't an easy time, but it was full of experiences and lessons that would shape her and help set her up for success in the future. Sarah moved back to Michigan in 1999. She wondered what her next steps would be in order to fill some of the gaps from her busy life in LA. It was a humbling time for her as she had to start over in so many ways. One consistent thread in moving back was staying involved in the Auto Show circuit, and she continued that for another five years. Not long after moving back, in 2001, she met James Schneider. As she got to know him, she was impressed with his kind heart, independence, and entrepreneurial spirit. James was extremely hard working and built a successful industrial cleaning and demolition business from the ground up. When he was starting out, he would pick workers up off the streets in Detroit in his van and pay them an hourly wage to make sure that he had enough of a crew to complete his jobs. He hustled over the years to build something from scratch and the company grew exponentially.

Early on, one of the things that James and Sarah would talk about when they would get together was how important it is to be in a space that makes you feel good. A space that is warm and aesthetically pleasing. They definitely had this in common. They would talk about different businesses that would be fun and satisfying to start, businesses that would make a difference in the community. Sarah saw that James was also a dreamer and a creator, and that he was willing to work hard to bring things into reality. Sarah and James' relationship grew, and they were married in 2003. They started their married life in Waterford, Michigan, but it took time for them to have children. During this period, Sarah started to become very interested in photography. She had always appreciated art, but she went to a conference in California and saw the business side of photography and thought that she could really do this in her community. Shortly after returning, she got set up and focused on lifestyle, family, newborns, and senior photography. As her business grew, blogging and Instagram was becoming a mainstream way to communicate. Sarah also saw that this could be another kind of business. In this way, she could combine her love for photography and design and express herself in a new and exciting way. Still living in Waterford, Sarah and James had a carriage house over their garage. Sarah created a plan to convert it into a guest suite.

It was a tiny space, but she poured herself into it to make it special. Through the fall season, Sarah was working hard to get it ready for James' brother and his family, their first guests during that Thanksgiving holiday. Just as they arrived, Sarah was literally putting the last screw into a curtain rod bracket to hold the drapes. All of her work had paid off and she had created an amazing space. It was finally finished! Without hesitation, they greeted their family guests, put their bags in the carriage house, and prepared to have Thanksgiving dinner.

As everyone came downstairs, Sarah realized that she didn't take a picture of her creation. She excused herself quickly and ran back to the carriage house with her iPhone. The first thing that hit her when she got upstairs was that it was dark outside. Without natural light, she didn't feel that she could take the best picture. Without another option, she took the picture, edited it quickly, and posted it on Instagram. Sarah didn't have many Instagram followers at that time, but they all loved her carriage house picture, and she was having great fun expressing herself with what she had brought to life. About two weeks later, her phone started to go crazy with notifications. She didn't understand what was happening. She went into her Instagram account and saw thousands and thousands of followers being added to her account. She soon saw that Anthropologie, her number one source for inspiration in home décor and fashion, had reposted her picture to their site. Within an instant, and without any notice, millions of people were viewing her carriage house picture. Sarah reached out to Anthropologie to talk to them about what was happening with this picture. She was hoping to get a discount off of their products to make it easier for her to do more projects. When she got connected to the right person, she was informed that her picture was the number one most liked picture for that year! This led to a close working relationship with them, which brought more and more Anthropologie reposts. She has done many popular projects with Anthropologie, including a total interior redesign of a Gulf Stream travel trailer. Things continued to build and before Sarah knew it, she had a strong platform on Instagram leveraging one of the most popular brands in fashion. This event was a turning point for Sarah, as it gave her a tremendous amount of confidence. After being misunderstood in her early years, and then spending time in California making a way for herself, things started to come together for her and she began building serious momentum by just being herself. Today, Sarah has nearly 90,000 people following her journey of dreaming, designing, and creating on Instagram. Sarah and James were married for about four and a half years now and they had their first child. Not only was Sarah expressing herself on Instagram and through her photography business, but she was also honing her skills in entertaining in her home. She was bringing her dreams to life by creating special dinner party events that combined amazing food that she prepared with the right ambiance to make the experience special. She had a serious love for gathering and bringing people together and she was on a mission to get better and better at it. Sarah and James also had their eye on Clarkston as a possible place to live. It's a neighboring town to Waterford, where they spent time dreaming about the possibilities there. They felt that there was a lot of potential in Clarkston and they wanted to be part of it. Not long after, they made the decision to move there and make it their home. With Sarah wanting to do more and more in the community, and with James' love for business and investing, they started dreaming together on what their possibilities could be. They didn't exactly know what they were going to do, but a restaurant was definitely on the list. They started to put feelers out in the community to see what downtown commercial real estate was available for purchase.

As they started to network and discuss their idea of investing in downtown Clarkston, they were quickly and consistently told that nothing would become available to them. They came across some interesting properties, but they would need to be rezoned commercial. As they went down that path, they came to the conclusion that it was extremely difficult to rezone property downtown. This put them back to square one, but they weren't discouraged. They knew that something would open up for them. Two years had gone by as they continued looking. Surprisingly, they got a call from the Clarkston State Bank, which had their main branch location at 15 S. Main Street in downtown Clarkston. According to the Clarkston historical records (clarkstonhistory. Info/history/chd/buildings/mainsw_015. Htm), 15 S. Main Street had several different businesses located there in the late 1800s, but in 1912, the Clarkston Bank Exchange was formed and they built the handsome stone building that is there today. The building from 1912 on always served as a bank of some kind. The Clarkston State Bank was founded in 1999 as a local institution serving customers in Clarkston and Waterford. People weren't coming downtown to do their banking in person as much anymore and the bank was looking to sell this location. They asked Sarah and James to consider being part of the bidding process. The bank wanted to see the building being used in the community for something other than a bank. Sarah and James took a tour of the location and it was definitely set up as a bank with back-office space and teller locations in the front as you walked in. James saw the potential of investing in the building and Sarah imagined peeling back the layers and felt that she could create a space that would be perfect for a restaurant location—a timeless place where people could enjoy a special moment with friends, family, and business associates.

As things moved forward, it was interesting to Sarah that they didn't publicly put the building up for sale. They didn't even put a price on the building. The bank was very selective on who they asked to bid on the property. Because this would have been their first property, and Sarah and James didn't have an established name in the community for executing on a business venture of this type, Sarah felt that they were the obvious underdogs in the purchasing process. They stayed engaged, but they tempered their expectations around actually being awarded the winning bid. Some time had passed, and while on a ski trip in Colorado, Sarah received a simple message from the bank that said, "Please put your bid in on the bank building today, and state what you want to do with the location." Sarah was at the top of the mountain when she received the message. Being excited and nervous at the same time, she took a deep breath and skied down to the bottom and got to their condo as fast as she could. Without any time to spare, she was pulling her thoughts together in a mad rush. When she arrived, she opened her computer and started to express her dream to the sellers for developing the location. She shared her heart in a very simple and transparent way in order to convey how she was going to bring this location to life for the community. That same day, Sarah and James came to an agreement on what they wanted to pay for the property. With that last piece in place, before Sarah knew it, she sent the bid for the building along with her vision to turn the location into an amazing restaurant location. They received a wonderful response that their bid had been accepted! As they started the process of buying the building, a huge reality set in. They had just taken an enormous leap of faith into the unknown. Their vision was uncompromising, but what it would take to complete it would only unfold as they took each step forward.

THE FED COMMUNITY

The first step was to take Sarah's vision for the restaurant and create a story that would speak to what they were trying to accomplish. Along with this, they needed to create renderings of the building as to how they would transform the inside, while maintaining the historic integrity of the outside. Once they pulled all of this together, they began to present their plans to the Clarkston City Council, The Clarkston Historic Society, and the Clarkston Planning Committee. Because these three teams are charged with making sure that the historic charm lives on, they all needed to sign off on their project plans. This kicked off a three-year process as they worked together to sift through the plans, make adjustments, and eventually bring things to a final approval. What came out of this process for Sarah was a deep respect for what she was becoming a part of. Through the approval process, she felt that even though they weren't well known in Clarkston, when all of the approvals were done, she believed that they demonstrated that they were "all in" to help add to what drew them to Clarkston in the first place: that special historic hometown experience. In parallel to that process, Sarah was fine tuning the concept for the restaurant and brainstorming how her ideas would function in real life. Because she had never owned and operated this type of business, she couldn't draw from her past experience. As a result, she began going to restaurants near and far to imagine, compare, and gather information on what was working and not working for other people. The proposed main dining room had become planning central for décor, the kitchen, business operations, and drink and food menu approaches. Tear sheets full of ideas were plastered on the walls and Sarah had crafted her own space to create and dream, just like in her father's studio when she was young. Though it was a tremendous amount of work, there was a fire within her to see this project come to life. As they were in their third year of approvals with the community planning committees, Sarah was interviewing for the main chef and associated kitchen and wait staff. The work toward the end was exhausting and rewarding at the same time. Three years after the initial purchase of the building, Sarah could see the light at the end of the tunnel. The grand opening was a success, and they conducted several soft openings. They were now ready for prime time. In July of 2017, The Fed Community officially opened its doors. To Sarah's elation, people were eager to try their place out. Once they opened to the public, people came—and kept coming! Though opening The Fed was a major highlight and accomplishment in Sarah's life, there was also a tough side to it. As she looks back on their first year, there was no real way for her to prepare for how mean-spirited some people were with their critiques, some from people that never even stepped into their establishment. This project was something that she labored over and sacrificed with her heart and soul and now she was forced to build a filter to separate the constructive reviews from the harsh reviews. She wanted The Fed to succeed, so she welcomed feedback when they made mistakes or didn't meet people's expectations. She realized that this was a side of the business that she was initially unprepared for. It was painful at first, but over time, her proverbial exterior skin toughened and she was able to fully embrace the constructive ones and use them to enhance their operations. She also learned how to throw out everything that was unfounded or said just to try and tear them down.

The Fed's momentum started and never stopped. Two years had passed by and they were seeing very clearly what was working for them, and they were able to capitalize on it. They had found their stride and word of The Fed was spreading around the region and across the country. It had become known as an amazing place that you just had to try. In very short order, their restaurant had become part of the fabric of Clarkston and was now drawing people to the beautiful downtown area. Just as they were celebrating the accomplishments from all of their hard work and feeling confident that they would continue to win in every aspect of their plan, an unexpected global phenomenon arose: COVID-19. In March of 2020, this sickness was spreading across the county and all forms of fear started to fill the hearts and minds of people. The United States was not only suffering from the impact of the sickness, but without notice, mandates started sweeping across the state of Michigan and around the country. Mandates to wear masks, social distance, get vaccinated, and stop meeting in groups. For The Fed to survive, Sarah had to again dig deep and figure out, based on the rules of the day or month, what they could do and couldn't do to keep its doors open. As most every restaurant did in the country, they closed their dining room and focused on carryout orders. To serve the community, they creatively decided to pull together family style to-go menus based on the food supply that they could get their hands on. Then some days, they were forced to shut down entirely for unknown extended periods of time. This would cause them to shift directions at a moments' notice and figure out how they could get rid of their food supply before it spoiled. To fix this problem, they would send food home with the staff and donate it to those in need.

The hardest part for Sarah was how it impacted the incredible team that they had built up. For Sarah, they were part of her extended family and now she needed to figure out how to keep as many people as possible while staying afloat. It was a weighty day-to-day burden that her entire team carried. As things started to open up slowly, the next enormous hurdle for her was to work to expand her team again. The government had rushed in to provide aid to hurting people, but the aid began to backfire as people were making more money collecting unemployment benefits by staying at home, rather than coming back to work. Sarah had to find the best quality people that wanted to work even though they would make less doing so—and she did! She fought, and never stopped fighting, to keep her dream alive. She kept every ounce of her creative heart and mind engaged, and with the help of her team, loyal patrons, friends, and family, she was able to make a way through the pain, confusion, and fear of that time. The Fed adjusted to the new normal, and Sarah began dreaming again around the possibilities of what the future would hold for them. After being open for six years now, she has gained a tremendous amount of experience and insight into how to make The Fed operate more successfully. She went from having a dream, with little to no experience, to becoming a formidable operator in the restaurant business. She's created a unique environment that takes you away from the day-to-day stresses of life and brings you to a place of rest so that you can be present with your family, friends, and co-workers. The Fed has won the Clarkston Beautification Award for the incredible job that they did with the property, inside and out. Realtors have also contacted her to let her know that The Fed is part of what they show off when they are sharing what makes Clarkston a special place to live as they sell to prospective homeowners. With that, Sarah feels a tremendous sense of responsibility as a Clarkston business owner to be involved in the community. Some of her greatest memories of the past six years has been around being part of Clarkston in ways that she never imagined. She has a special place in her heart for Habitat for Humanity and for Clarkston Public Schools. Whenever the opportunity arises, she tries to make herself and The Fed available to help and support their community efforts. Sarah also supports local non-profit organizations by providing a location where they can host their annual fundraisers. All of this has provided a platform for Sarah and her team. It gives them an opportunity to give from their hearts, which in turn creates a greater connection for them into the community. This connection helps them see where they can give in the future. She wants to see Clarkston continue to flourish as a community. Their family has grown and James and Sarah now have three children that have been part of their entrepreneurial journey. With the growth of their business and associated successes in hand, Sarah continues to dream about what's next. Sarah and James have purchased additional properties in downtown Clarkston with the hopes of bringing some new businesses into the community. Her creative juices are flowing with a richer and more comprehensive understanding of how she can support Clarkston's growth moving forward.

ENTREPRENEURIAL INSIGHTS

When you spend time with Sarah, you quickly realize that she is a force of encouragement. She seems to continually see the possibilities in people and in situations. Here are a few insights that make her an effective entrepreneur.

KNOWING WHO YOU ARE (14-IDENTITY)

Sarah has a strong internal sense of who she is and who she isn't. Even as a child, she gravitated to art and design and had an inherent sense of what attributes made a room, or a space, special. When others didn't understand her, she gravitated toward people that did. In a world where everyone seems to be comparing themselves to someone else, Sarah has a distinct connection with who she is as a person and she celebrates it. In Sarah's world, being a unique artistic dreamer is good.

WILLING TO GO ALL IN TO MAKE HER DREAMS COME TO LIFE (15-DREAM)

Sarah has a unique quality in that she is able to align comprehensive action plans to her dreams in order to see them come to life. We all know dreamers that don't seem to accomplish much. That is not how Sarah is wired. Her world doesn't become complete until she sees her dreams materialize. Once she has crafted her plan, she goes all in to see it come to pass. Throughout her past—from making and selling soap dishes, moving to LA, creating a photography business, getting established on Instagram, to bringing The Fed to life—Sarah continues to demonstrate significant impact in association with her dreams because she is willing to go all in to bring things to life.

STAY THE COURSE (16-STAY)

Once Sarah's plan is in place, she rarely moves off course. Her creativity allows for a flow that takes in the possibilities of optimizing things on a day-to-day basis, but Sarah stays on target no matter what. Bringing the dream to reality, regardless of the obstacles that come in front of her, is a fierce part of who Sarah is. Her early years of dreaming, staying on track, and overcoming obstacles shaped her for the future. Whether it was working through the long three-year process of opening The Fed or overcoming COVID-19, she stayed the course to keep her dreams alive.

PRESSURE CAN BRING GREATER DEPTHS OF CREATIVITY (17-CREATIVITY)

The pressure that is created when you have a big dream and you step into the unknown can be profound. Sarah told me that if she had known how difficult following her dreams would have been at times, she probably would have contemplated dreaming another dream to avoid the hardship. Each time that she overcame, however, she gained more confidence, courage, and faith in herself. Instead of the pressure pushing her down, she came out of it with a greater depth of creativity to dream a bigger dream. Overcoming the pressure of her circumstances propelled her forward, not backward.

CHAPTER FIVE

LEGACY SUSTAINING GROWTH

The Stoll Family Story

PEOPLE GROW UP in a family business environment and understand that someday they are going to help lead the company into the future. When that time does come, due to market place pressures, everything that made the company successful in the past won't carry them solely into the future. The challenge now becomes how to leverage what they have and forge into new unknown areas to keep the business relevant, alive, and flourishing.

The Stoll family has been on that exact journey. With humble beginnings, at the age of 55 in 1969, William Stoll handcrafted an oversized metal screen for the fireplace in his new home. Seeing that he could make and market fireplace screens and doors to the local community to help support his family, the Stoll family business was formed, initially as Stoll Fireplace, Inc. Stoll Industries, headquartered in Abbeville, South Carolina, is now in its third generation. With over 1800 independent dealers across the country, they provide decorative metal products for every room, inside and outside, of the home. Their journey over the last fifty years demonstrates a powerful and authentic business approach that incorporates how they build and maintain their culture, address significant market challenges, innovate into new markets, serve the needy, and dream big dreams for the future.

HISTORY AND BACKGROUND: FIRST GENERATION

William Stoll was originally from Virginia Beach, Virginia. Born in 1914, he lost his mother at the early age of four to the Flu Pandemic of 1918. During the pandemic, an estimated 50 million people died around the world. This death toll rose to a number greater than those who lost their lives in World War I. Many that experienced this type of loss, in the midst of such hard times, were driven to bitterness. This hardship, however, seemed to push William into being extremely compassionate to the needs of people. Growing up in a Mennonite farming community in Virginia Beach, William demonstrated a keen ability to create and invent with metal. When there was a practical need on the farm or within the community, he could visualize a solution and then go into his metal shop and bring it to life. For example, with the water table being high in the area, flooding was an issue. William envisioned a solution and built a three-point hitch attachment for the back of the tractor that leveraged three paddles to produce a furrow or trench that was used to help control the water in the field. In raising small cucumbers to become pickles, it was back-breaking work to harvest them off of the vines that grew on the surface of the ground. As a result, William designed and built a machine that included a platform that was low to the ground that allowed six men to hover over the vines so that they could more easily pick the cucumbers and toss them into a bin. From there, a conveyor would sort them so that people on top of the machine could put them in baskets.

He had a passion to create and invent things that would make life better for people. He wanted to take burdens away from people, not just invent things to make money for himself. Coupled with William's creativity was an adventurous spirit. He loved to travel and even created a pop-up camper to better accommodate his family trips. In every area of his life, he was looking to create and invent to improve things. He believed in living life to the fullest and found a way to integrate his favorite pastimes into his long work day. If he wanted to go fishing, he would wake up at 4:00 am to get an early start on his day so that he could make sure that he got his fishing time in. William created a work hard, play hard environment that seemed to fuel his creativity and his ability to dream. This environment also kept the door open for friends and family to find a place in William's life so that he could learn and grow, but also nurture and mentor others. During the mid '60s, it became evident to William that as the city of Virginia Beach was expanding into the rural communities, it was restricting their ability to expand their operations and grow. He decided that it was time to investigate the possibility of moving his family to another area so that they could continue to prosper. William was on a land selection committee and started traveling into South Carolina looking for a new beginning. For himself, it wasn't just for farming; he wanted to see his metal working business grow and expand also. At the age of 55 in 1969, he found a great piece of property with his brother and cousin in Abbeville, South Carolina, and made an offer that was accepted. As he traveled back to let his family know that they would be moving, the real estate person informed him that the wife of the couple that had accepted his offer was in great distress over the sale and asked if he would let them out of the deal. Moved with compassion, William immediately released them from the deal without hesitation. Impacted by his great generosity, the real estate agent approached a significant land owner in the area and told him about what had just happened. He asked the land owner if he would be willing to sell some of his land to the Stoll family. Shortly after, a new deal was struck to acquire 500 acres of prime farm land with a beautiful 7-acre pond on the property.

The Stolls' move to Abbeville became the foundation and launching pad for his legacy. When he moved into his new home, he realized that there wasn't a screen protector on the irregularly shaped fireplace. He went to the hardware store to purchase a screen, but he couldn't find anything that would fit. Seeing that he couldn't find an easy solution to his problem, he went into his shop and built a high-quality, good looking custom screen. Word spread in the local community about his craft and he built some for his neighbors, and eventually sold them out of the local hardware store. In 1969, Stoll Fireplace was created and they began serving the local community with quality fireplace products. As fuel prices started to rise in the 1970s and fuel conservation became top of mind, he also designed and built wood stoves for a time. Early on, William's reputation for being an excellent craftsman and dealing with customers and suppliers with high integrity became a significant part of his reputation. He sincerely cared about other people and would often times put others first over his own personal needs. His work ethic and genuine sincerity to care for other people was infectious and it was a core principle on how he ran the company. His Christian faith was a practical code of honor on how to live and how to treat people with dignity and respect. He was honest, direct, and compassionate. His hope was not only to provide for his family, but to also share the profits with the poor and the needy. Though the profits were slim in the early years, this foundational principle would shape future generations. William fought long and hard to establish this young company. There were many times when they were just getting by, but William pushed forward to keep the company alive with the help and support of his family.

SECOND GENERATION

The company grew and expanded in the local region throughout the '70s and into the '80s. In the mid '80s, William sold the business to his five sons and his son-in-law. Under new ownership, this young team kept providing products in the hearth industry, but they also ventured out into new areas in order to grow the company and help keep the slow summers profitable. One of their new products that they brought to market was the Stoll utility trailer. At that time, most of the manufacturing of trailers was done in the central region of the US, like Texas and Oklahoma. Because of this, they were able to fill a production need on the East Coast and their sales began to take off. They also manufactured metal bubble gum machine stands by the thousands, as well as cattle catchers in order to service the local community. Anything that they could manufacture to expand the business and increase revenue was an option for them. Though these products didn't continue to be produced long-term, it demonstrated the tenacity of the Stolls to be creative and branch out into new areas in order to grow and sustain their young company. Though they were growing and expanding, after three years, it became apparent to the six stakeholders that there were too many people weighing in on the day-to-day decisions. They also saw that the small business was not large enough to sustain all of the families that were involved. As a result, two of William's sons, Dennis and Robert, decided to buy out their three brothers and their brother-in-law. This wasn't a surprise, as growing up, Dennis and Robert did everything together. They were inseparable. Both of them were very adventurous, and each one brought a key contribution to the business. Dennis had a vision for the art of the possible regarding the expansion of the business and bringing new products into the company. When brainstorming new products, Robert could see the product in his mind, how to create it, and then how to optimize the process for manufacturing. This complementary team effort became a differentiator for them in the marketplace as they were able to listen to the needs of their customers and bring new products to market with an approach to manufacturing that enhanced their profitability.

During the rest of the '80s, they were positioned for success, but the economy was in a downturn. At times, the business would slow down to a standstill and the brothers would have to decide if they wanted to move forward or disband. These were difficult times for them, but at the end of each conversation, they would agree to keep pushing forward and to stay together. Because of their humility, work ethic, and determination in these difficult times, the bank, their suppliers, and even their father, would extend payment terms to help keep their company moving forward. Good to their word, as things would pick up, they were quick to bring their accounts current. These difficult times stretched them significantly, but while they were being stretched, a great resolve to see the company grow and expand was being deposited inside of them. They wanted to see the number of products increase in the market, but now they also wanted to see their impact grow across the country. After five years, the second generation of Stolls were well on their way and beginning to find their stride. As they entered the '90s, Dennis took responsibility for expanding their product mix, as well as expanding their network into new markets. The first Stoll Industries sales representative was hired as they challenged themselves to think bigger. With this growth and product expansion, Robert was challenged with creating multiple products at the same time, optimizing the manufacturing process, and expanding their physical manufacturing footprint. In the beginning, they repurposed existing buildings to manufacture new products and it worked well for them as they grew. They were both being stretched again, but in a way where they could start to see more of their potential. They admitted to themselves that they were over their heads in many situations, but they bounced ideas off of each other and brainstormed solutions that made it apparent that they were becoming a great team. They also started to see that as they established and maintained high-quality trusting relationships, and as they produced products with high quality for a better price, their differentiation became clear to them and very apparent to the marketplace. As they were getting their company's house in order and working together in a more productive way, a very influential distributor from their area came to them to have them produce a unique product just for him and his network of dealers. With that opportunity, it opened a significant amount of dealer relationships on the East Coast that jump started their network beyond anything that they could have done on their own. Because they entered an exclusive deal with this distributor for three years, they were able to establish themselves as a premier manufacturer that had very high-quality standards and was easy to do business with. When the contract period expired, they were able to take their business relationships directly to these same dealers, which further enhanced their network and associated profitability. The fact that the distributor had treated them with honesty and integrity, just as they had been treating their customers and suppliers, they started to see that that they were attracting people with similar values. This in turn was helping them expand toward having a national influence. This experience showed them that marketing directly to dealers, versus going through distributors, worked well for them and that they wanted to leverage this model whenever possible. This strategy gave them the ability to expand while avoiding risk by having a multitude of sales channels instead of a few through distributors. For the first time, they were building momentum financially and they started to have excess capital to invest in the business instead of exclusively leveraging bank notes. This new financial freedom also gave them the ability to passionately give to the humanitarian charities that were important to them. They set this as a strategic part of their business, believing that they had a responsibility to give to others that were less fortunate. In the '90s, the hearth industry had a few really big players dominating the market. Stoll Industries was still very small compared to the large influencers of the day. When they would go to trade shows, people would recognize them more as a new player, trying to break into the market. As the Stolls continued to build momentum, they became known as a company that was honest, provided great products, and was willing to look out for the interests of all parties involved. In that day, some of the big national manufacturers would require dealers to buy a large amount of product each year in order to keep their dealer status active. If the market was down in that particular year, they were forced to buy the same amount of product the next year, putting an undue burden on the dealer's business. Because of this reality, the Stolls started to offer flexible purchasing agreements to their dealers. This gave Stoll Industries another differentiator in the market while putting their dealers in a better position overall.

Each level of expansion was a stretching and growth experience for Dennis and Robert. From where they started, in the humble beginnings of their father's local business, some decisions that they made from their naivety were less productive. William, Dennis, and Robert stayed humble. They resisted, even in their successes, the inclination that they knew it all. This gave them a profound place to stay teachable. With a high school education, they felt that this was their university training and they wanted to take advantage of every teachable moment. As a result, they were open to consider every idea that was passed to them. This allowed them to have many counselors from the industry giving them insights as to what would make them more successful. For example, one large influential dealer out of Ohio saw that their product marketing needed work, so he coached them in invaluable ways. When they realized that they could have done better in a deal, they agreed to honor their agreement and trust that other opportunities would open up for them. It was a painful process at times, but they realized that it was better for them to honor their business principles rather than break a commitment. This approach worked out well for them because, as is in business, there are people watching how you do business, even when you don't know they are watching. This further built their loyalty brand, and people knew that when you do business with Stoll Industries, they will hold up their end of the bargain. They learned from every experience and their brand loyalty more than made up for the mistakes that they made.

THE TEN-YEAR TRANSITION

With their foundation set, they entered the 2000s with significant momentum. They had a stellar brand; they had created a national network of suppliers and dealers, as well as a team of strong field reps; they had a sound and proven approach to product development; and they had a mature and dependable manufacturing footprint. With a seat firmly at the table in the industry, they were able to better negotiate their position and increase their profitability, which greatly increased their influence in the market. Between 2008 and 2009, Dennis and Robert felt that it was time to start a transition of the ownership of the business to the next generation. In talking with key business leaders that had transitioned family businesses successfully to the next generation, they decided to adopt a ten-year transition plan. This plan consisted of identifying family members that would be successful in certain roles. Once identified, Dennis, Robert, and members of the management team would mentor them over time in the day-to-day business affairs of that role so that when it was time to cut over, everyone would be prepared. Five family members that had a passion for the business were identified to be part of the future leadership team: Darris Stoll, President and CEO; Gary Yoder, VP of Sales and Marketing; Doug Stoll, VP of Operations; Jonathon Stoll, Director of Engineering; and Weston Stoll, Process Engineer. All of the family members started working in the business early on and they had the benefit of being part of the company culture. Integrated into the hard work—which consisted of seventy, eighty, and ninety hours per week—was a light-hearted, humorous work environment that rarely missed an opportunity to bring levity to the day. It was a place that people wanted to be. This strong bond of working hard and enjoying the relationships with each other was a key part of William's work lifestyle, and something that Dennis and Robert embraced and brought forward. Each new management team member had an opportunity to see the cultural values played out in front of them as they prepared for their future role, not as a list of rules, but as a living, breathing code that differentiated them in the industry. As the company continued to grow, expand across the country, expand their product mix outside of the hearth industry, and accumulate valuable market share, they could see with their own eyes as to why the company had been built on honesty, integrity, and honor. As the transition progressed, while sitting in their future roles, they also could see what was working well and what could be improved. Seeing Dennis and Robert as examples of students of change, they were expected to make things better as they learned the company. They were told by Dennis and Robert, "Just because this is the way that we do it now doesn't mean it's the best way moving forward. Listen to your co-workers, your dealers, your suppliers, and your trusted advisors and do what makes sense to grow the business in the current market without compromising our company values."

THIRD GENERATION

In 2019, the transition was complete. Stoll Fireplace, Inc. became Stoll Industries, Inc. and officially had its third generation of leaders. The operations of the company had been in the hands of the new management team and things were running smoothly. Dennis and Robert were available to give them counsel when needed, but they started to stay a healthy distance away from the new team so that everyone could get settled into their new roles. Dennis and Robert knew that their leadership roles had been transferred successfully and they made a commitment not to challenge or second-guess the new management team. William hadn't done it to them, and they were committed to follow on with that example. Once the management team was in place, they moved to enhance some key components of their culture. One of the first things they did was to put a non-profit 501c3 entity, Stoll Cares, in place to formally position their giving culture as a focal point for the company. With every product sold, Stoll contributes money into Stoll Cares in order to support those less fortunate around the world. This also gives them the opportunity to receive contributions from their business network to further enhance their outreach to help others. Another thing that they brought forward was integrating their wives into the decision-making process of the company. The insights that their spouses are contributing are giving them a more comprehensive approach to solving problems. They are at the beginning stages of this, but they are excited to see how it will mature moving forward. They are also working hard to cut back on overtime with their employees to help cultivate a better work-life balance environment. They have a long way to go, but they believe that they are on the right track. Their hope is to see their company become more of a community. Not just a place where products are manufactured and sold, but a place where they can better celebrate their victories together and face life's challenges together as an extended family. One of the strengths of their multi-generational business is that they had a tremendous amount of experience in their field with a proven track record. As they grew, it became apparent to the new management team that they needed more input from outside experts to speak into how they were managing their operations and their people and how to function more effectively as a management team. Regarding their operations, the state of South Carolina offered a program around lean manufacturing. Lean manufacturing approaches the reduction of waste, focuses on customer value, and seeks to achieve continuous process improvement. The program provided training and consulting to the company that would prove to be an invaluable investment. In addition to this, the program also gave them insights and an approach to map out career paths for all of their employees. This way, employees know what it will take to improve in their role, as well as understand what it will take to receive promotions and raises. Bringing a transparent framework to their over one hundred employees has strengthened the already strong culture that was in place. As they entered into 2020, things were running smoothly and they were starting to gel as a new management team. Their business was continuing to grow and everything was looking up for them. Rumors of COVID-19 were starting to surface early in the year, and by March of 2020, they started to feel the impact of their dealers closing their stores. By the end of April, the sales from their dealer network almost went down to zero. In the face of the unknown, they drew together as a management team and refused to fall into fear. Darris explains, "We rely on our beliefs around faith, prayer, and practical trust in a divine Creator to give us literal guidance in day-to-day operational strategy and product design." Like the management teams that came before them, they asked God for insight into their unknown circumstances. There wasn't a playbook for what they were facing and they needed to move decisively and with confidence. Three key decisions came out of their intense prayer and brainstorming sessions. The first thing that became clear to them was to keep their employees financially whole and pay them their full hourly rate even though production was all but shut down. The second thing was to prepare for growth. They had a strong sense that their business was going to rebound quickly and they wanted to be ready for it. The third thing that they decided was to aggressively implement their lean manufacturing strategy in order to streamline their manufacturing footprint and get their production under one roof. The issue that they had on this topic was that, as they grew over the last twenty years, they would repurpose farm buildings or build new structures to accommodate new product lines. When they were busy, they didn't realize how inefficient their manufacturing process had become. When the pandemic hit and everything stopped, they could more clearly see that they needed to get all of their production under one roof. The other thing that worked in their favor is that they had the paid manpower to get the job done.

As they got started dismantling their old production footprint and continued to pray for guidance, they felt an urgency to get their new production facility installed and tested by the 4th of July. They decided to have their crew design and build equipment whenever possible to leverage the manpower that they were paying for. This included designing and building powder coating, paint, and sandblasting booths. They basically had four months to get everything production ready, and with tremendous teamwork, they accomplished their goal.

Their timing was impeccable, because as they finished completing their new manufacturing facility, their orders started coming in again. In fact, they have been running 20-30 percent over their orders from the same time the previous year, and it hasn't stopped to date. If they hadn't strategically reworked their manufacturing approach, they wouldn't have been able to keep up with the new demand. With the new business, they were planning to add on to their new production facility. By continuously improving their operations, however, they were able to leverage their existing space and avoid the time and expense of adding on. From a supply chain disruption perspective, they have surprisingly not met with much of a problem in this area.

In embracing William's vendor relationship strategy from day one, which was to treat every supplier with honor and respect, they have been building a tremendous amount of goodwill over the last fifty years with their supplier network. William, Dennis, and Robert stayed loyal to their suppliers and valued the long-term relationships where they wouldn't switch just to get a better price. If shipments were a little short or minorly damaged in transit, they would let their supplier know, but they wouldn't "nickel and dime" them for refunds, knowing that the supplier would take care of them when they needed help on their end. As constraints were being placed on the flow of materials in the industry, they found without even asking that their suppliers were giving them preference in order to keep their production up and running smoothly. When materials were stuck in ports around the country and the threat of delays were upon them, the shipments would mysteriously show up just in time to keep production running. With their new growth, they needed to add skilled tradesmen to handle the increased load. With other plants closing around them, their culture and brand within the region drew the right people at the right time to take their production team to the next level. Now on the other side of the pandemic, to keep their company transformation moving forward, they also brought in a management consultant, Ford Taylor, that focuses on leadership training and consulting and brings insights on how to protect the generational investment that they've made as a family. Ford has helped them define the legacy of Stoll Industries and what they want it to be moving forward, as it relates to their company, suppliers, dealers, and the community at large. As the leadership team embraced this approach, they also realized that they needed to get their families involved in the transformation. Even though the dynamics between the families were positive and healthy, they didn't have a structured approach in place for conflict resolution. Ford gave them tools, processes, and strategies to help them get issues on the table and not suppress things. He helped them deal with issues in a constructive manner so they could put things to rest and move on to strategic priorities in order to keep building and growing as individuals and as a company.

William Stoll embodied the heart of the craftsman. His legacy has been carried on through to each generation from 1969 to the present day. Serving people by building and distributing high-quality products with honesty, integrity, and honor is the cornerstone of the Stoll family business. William started building a simple fireplace screen, and today Stoll Industries produces an extensive array of hearth products, kitchen and bath products, outdoor living products, shelves and mantles, range hoods, cabinet facings, fireplace kits, and wall systems. They provide products for every walk of life, from people that live in one-room homes to people that live in the most elaborate high-rise establishments in Manhattan, New York. They have their sites on the globe, and with the foundation that they've built, there's no doubt that they will excel at that, as well.

ENTREPRENEURIAL INSIGHTS

Having a business that is successful in one person's lifetime is quite a feat. To have that company grow and thrive over three generations is extremely uncommon. I believe that the entrepreneurial insights that I've highlighted point to some key things that help identify what the Stolls have done to protect their legacy business.

CULTURE OF HONOR (18-CULTURE)

One of the biggest buzz words in the country today is "culture." You hear people talking about building a culture, influencing a culture, transforming a culture, integrating cultures, and it goes on and on. There is a renaissance going on in the world relating to people and culture. Remote work is increasing, there is a shortage of people in many sectors, there is a significant influx in compensation, and there is a significant influence, more than ever before, from a strong entitlement mindset that is taking place around work-life balance. With all of these new realities and associated headwinds, what the Stolls have been able to accomplish is pretty amazing regarding their culture. They have created a culture that is consistent inside and outside of their company. They don't have a list of rules to follow; they have a code of what they are pursuing to be as individuals. Darris said, "We truly treat people with honor, respect, dignity, and real love. We truly operate every part of our business in a way that cares for others and allows them to prosper." From the highest office to the most inexperienced employee, they embrace humility to listen, learn, and execute their plan. This builds an incredible bond of trust and helps create a healthy work environment. As they pursue this journey transparently, meaning that no one is perfect and everyone has a potential to grow and learn, they are able to focus on key issues within the business instead of being embroiled in cultural disfunction. This draws the best people to their company, creates the greatest relationships with their suppliers, and creates an environment of creativity that is allowing them to listen to the market and respond with an amazing result that is represented in their products. By treating people with respect, dignity, and honesty first, before focusing solely on profits, they are playing the long game in investing in people inside and outside of the company, especially those that are less fortunate.

DREAM BIG AND ACT ON IT (19-BIG)

I see each generation with a big dream and acting on it. For William, he dreamed of having more opportunity and was willing to pick up from Virginia Beach and relocate his family to South Carolina. For Dennis and Robert, they dreamed of taking the company from a local operation of eight employees to a national company with a much broader product portfolio. For Darris and his team, they dreamed of further expanding the company outside of the hearth industry to include kitchen and bath, outdoor living, home décor, and beyond. All these dreams at their inception were just dreams, but as they put actions to their plans and followed their dreams, doors opened and they took advantage of them in the best way that they could. When current market conditions seemed to delay their success, they waited it out and trusted in their plan. I find that there are typically dreamers and doers in the marketplace. To find the combination of both isn't common, but when it's in action, it tends to produce great results. The Stolls are great examples of this.

TESTED IN CHALLENGES (20-TESTED)

I rarely see a transition of leadership go by without some form of testing that takes place, whether its inside politics or market conditions or both. There always seems to be a mix of attitudes that need to be worked out from those that are skeptical, fearful, and neutral about the changes. Within a family business, because everyone knows each other and has most likely grown up with each other, it can be especially challenging to establish yourself in your new role. People can be skeptical of new leaders right up until they prove themselves in a difficult situation. Challenging times allow leaders the opportunity to build momentum by demonstrating that they are ready for what is coming their way. Most recently, as much as they had a brilliant plan to transition over a ten-year period of time, this last management team didn't escape the testing. Because of their commitment to themselves and staying true to their cultural values, they successfully weathered the storms of the management transition, a global pandemic, and significant growth. Stronger than ever, they will no doubt overcome each challenge that comes their way—together.

STAYING RELEVANT (21-RELEVANT)

I personally think that one of the greatest challenges that people face when they are counting their experiences in decades, not months or years, of accomplishments in business is in actually staying relevant to what's happening in the current environment. Have you ever been with people that have been in business for thirty or forty years and all that they talk about is "the good old days" or what they worked on that changed the world ten years ago? It's easy to become an expert in the things that used to be, instead of remaining a student of what might be coming next. There is a humility, a curiosity, and a hunger that works together inside of a person that challenges them to stay relevant to the things around them. In talking with Dennis Stoll, he mentioned that his family of leaders to date, including himself, have high school educations. He said that Stoll Industries is their college experience and they don't want to miss an opportunity to learn every day and do things better. His humility, curiosity, and hunger to win keeps him listening for what's next. His openness to listen to outside advisors challenged him to think beyond his personal experiences. I spoke to Darris, and in another example, he had decided to take the emphasis off a product line, let's call it product line A. He wanted to shift the focus to a product line that he felt had a greater potential, and we'll call that product line B. When working with a couple of dealers from a western state recently, without knowing what Darris had decided, they told him that whatever you do, don't take the emphasis off product line A. In listening to his network, he challenged himself to see the situation through their eyes and kept the emphasis on product line A. In doing so, that product line is taking off and product line B hasn't done as well as he had hoped. This team knows that they are only as good as their next best decision and they want to make the greatest impact that they can every day. In thinking like this, especially as they are expanding and growing significantly, they are bringing in key advisors and consultants that are helping them to make strategic decisions for the future. The Stolls are humble, curious, hungry... unstoppable!

SECTION 2

THE GROWTH CHALLENGE

IF YOU WERE to ask those who have accomplished great things the secret of their success, like winning the most valuable player (MVP) in football or winning the famed Pulitzer Prize, they will most likely tell you that it's never just one thing. It's several things that work together, and many of them are out of your control. When I was young, someone told me that great leaders are made, not born. I refuted that in my mind at the time, but after several decades in business, I do see solidly that great leaders are made, and made over time.

I've taken all of the entrepreneurial impacts from the five stories and created one word for each impact, that in my mind, provide an array of words that you can use to better yourself as you move along your journey. Some people are ready to launch into their next business adventure and form a new company. Some people are seated well within their career and they want to take their game to the next level. Some people may be in their older years and realize that there is more left for them to accomplish. A lot of times, we focus so much on where we want to go that we don't dig in and work on a consistent daily routine of honing in on business skills that will make us better at what we do. I suggest you take the time and think about what each word means to you and how you want to improve in that area. After doing that, I suggest that you select one word that you really want to grow and develop in. Make a decision to develop those attributes. Identify someone that you want to be like in this area. Pick someone that you esteem. Align your words, internally and externally, with what you want to accomplish, and confide in someone that you trust, within your business eco system, and let them know that you want to grow in this area. Give them permission to give you candid feedback on your journey to be better. Be vulnerable with them and give them permission over time to let you know how you are doing in that area. When they see that you are accomplished in that area, you most likely are. Self-assessing isn't the best way to grow, as we need feedback from others to make sure that we have a more well-rounded perspective in our journey to better ourselves. I encourage you to be transparent with others and humble yourself to accept insights from others. Growth is a team sport, and over time, if you let people in to help you grow, you will be sought after for your leadership, and I believe that you will become invaluable to the market place moving forward.

I've provided a chart within the growth challenge for each of the twenty-one words that I call a growth matrix. Within the matrix, there are three columns that I've labeled "Unproductive," "Productive," and "Accomplished" with examples of what each column represents. Across each column, there is a four-category rating scale that will allow you to rate where you are now on your growth journey, with an opportunity to also mark how you want to grow in the weeks and months ahead. You will notice that the rating scale allows you to straddle each category on your journey to becoming more mature. For example, you may mark yourself as a "3" for a word because you are performing as a "Productive" person, but you are also demonstrating maturity in the "Accomplished" column. Be transparent and mark where you are today on this scale as you consider what you want to adopt in the next category. Of course, I've provided a growth challenge that gives you a place to start. The goal will be for you to define your personal maturity goals by defining the things that you want to accomplish. One caveat: do not give yourself a 3 if you are presently demonstrating any of the "Unproductive" behaviors. Unproductive behaviors must be absent to rate yourself a 3 or 4. All the best to you as you press into your journey to grow and develop!

1

RESPECT

BEING RESPECTED AS a leader is not an easy feat to accomplish. One leader told me early in my career that you can always tell if you are a true leader: just turn around and see who is following you. If no one is following you, then maybe you have more work to do.

People are motivated in many different ways to respect you. John McMullen drew respect from his leaders, peers, and team because he was a high performer, and he wanted to see everyone around him perform at their highest level. He didn't motivate people with fear, empty promises, or the "what have you done for me lately" approach; he motivated them with high standards and his personal investment in each individual. When they succeeded, he did his part by giving them recognition and paid them well for their contribution. He made a deal with each team member and honored his part of the bargain without exception when they reached their goals.

CHALLENGE:

- Circle the actions that others say you demonstrate consistently.

- Place an X beside those actions you are not demonstrating consistently at this time.
- Place a box around the number in the growth matrix that best represents where you are today in your growth journey.
- Identify one action that you want to pursue in order to grow in this area.

<table>
<tr><th>UNPRODUCTIVE</th><th colspan="2">PRODUCTIVE</th><th>ACCOMPLISHED</th></tr>
<tr><td>1</td><td>2</td><td>3</td><td>4</td></tr>
<tr><td>• I demonstrate a lack of concern for others.
• I focus mostly on results and am not mindful of the methods.
• I show up every day to put in my time and get a paycheck.</td><td colspan="2">• I honor my word and hold to my agreements.
• I have a solid work ethic and lead by example.
• I do my best to contribute each day.</td><td>• I look out for the well-being of others while driving toward my goal.
• I recognize and reward others for their contribution.
• I bring out the best in others so that they perform at higher levels.</td></tr>
</table>

2

TEAM

I DON'T JUST WANT to define what a team is; I want to demonstrate how one works well in business. Being part of a team can be a very rewarding experience, and it can also be equally frustrating, depending on your circumstances.

What seems to make it rewarding, as seen in John's example, is when there is a team leader that is respected, there is a team goal that makes good business sense and is attainable, each team member has an area of contribution that helps the team function properly, there is a mutual trust and respect between team members, there is a willingness to sacrifice as a team in order to achieve the desired outcome, and there is a reward that is appropriate for each team member when the team achieves its goals. This is not an exhaustive list, but it does represent some key attributes of a high performing team.

Low performing teams, on the other hand, lack some of the items listed above. They also include leaders that only care about themselves, team members that are strong individual contributors but can't or won't work with others, and high-profile team members that don't carry their weight and rely on others to do their work. These are just a few and I'm sure that I've touched a nerve with you!

CHALLENGE:

- Circle the actions that others say you demonstrate consistently.
- Place an X beside those actions you are not demonstrating consistently at this time.
- Place a box around the number in the growth matrix that best represents where you are today in your growth journey.
- Identify one action that you want to pursue in order to grow in this area.

<table>
<tr><th colspan="2">UNPRODUCTIVE</th><th colspan="2">PRODUCTIVE</th><th colspan="2">ACCOMPLISHED</th></tr>
<tr><td>1</td><td colspan="2">2</td><td colspan="2">3</td><td>4</td></tr>
<tr><td colspan="2">• I care only about my individual contribution.
• I lack the connection to how my contribution impacts others.
• I manipulate others to do my work for me.</td><td colspan="2">• I understand that everyone's contribution is important to attain the overall goal.
• I operate with an understanding of how each member's contribution impacts the overall team goal.
• I show up every day with my "A-Game" contribution.</td><td colspan="2">• I foster a culture of trust and transparency.
• I sacrifice to help other team members win.
• I recognize and praise the accomplishments of other team members.</td></tr>
</table>

3

GIVER

HAVE YOU HAD the opportunity to be around a giver? Maybe you are one yourself. Obviously, the opposite of a giver is a miser: one who is extremely stingy with money. Have you had the unfortunate opportunity to work with a miser? Or maybe this is the type of person that you are today.

Even though John grew up with meager beginnings, he never let go of where he came from and the associated risks that he needed to overcome. John is a fierce competitor in all aspects of his life. In addition to his competitive spirit, he has a strong drive to help those who are in need.

A giver is someone that doesn't just throw resources around; they are thoughtful investors. The investment can be money, recognition, acknowledgements, endorsements, references, encouragement, mentoring, and many other things that help people improve their present situation. John knew that he was only as strong as the team that was around him. As a result, he was intentional about being a giver whenever the opportunity arose personally, in business, and in the community.

CHALLENGE:

- Circle the actions that others say you demonstrate consistently.

- Place an X beside those actions you are not demonstrating consistently at this time.
- Place a box around the number in the growth matrix that best represents where you are today in your growth journey.
- Identify one action that you want to pursue in order to grow in this area.

<table>
<tr><th colspan="4">UNPRODUCTIVE</th><th colspan="4">PRODUCTIVE</th><th colspan="4">ACCOMPLISHED</th></tr>
<tr><td colspan="3">1</td><td colspan="3">2</td><td colspan="3">3</td><td colspan="3">4</td></tr>
<tr><td colspan="4">• If I give to others, it compromises my chances of getting ahead.
• When I give to others, it makes them weak.
• No one helped me get ahead; therefore, I'm not going to help others.</td><td colspan="4">• I'm thankful for those that helped make a way for me to succeed and I honor them whenever I can.
• I look to help those around me personally and professionally.
• I publicly recognize the accomplishments of others when it doesn't benefit me.</td><td colspan="4">• I dedicate a percentage of my finances to help others in need.
• I take personal time to mentor people into being great leaders.
• I dedicate time to serve on boards and leadership teams of non-profit help organizations.</td></tr>
</table>

4

TIMING

I'M SURE THAT most people have heard the phrase, "Timing is everything." No one person can accurately predict the perfect timing for something all of the time. I've heard music artists say that they wrote a great song, but released it at the wrong time and didn't get the biggest impact from their audience. I've also heard business people say that they lost money on an investment because they got into a certain deal too late.

In reviewing John's experiences with timing related to key moments over his lifetime, he seemed to get it right more than he got it wrong. A few of the key elements that I've observed from his story is that he: 1) doesn't throw caution to the wind and guess, but rather owns the responsibility to get the timing right to the best of his ability, 2) has a keen attention to the details in his present situation (he keeps his head in the game), 3) has a growing wisdom from the school of "hard knocks" or learning from past mistakes, 4) has a small group of trusted expert counselors that help weigh in on the decision, and 5) has the ability to take the risk to act and own the end result, being good or bad... always being a student to learn and do better next time. Mastering the practice of timing will serve you well in everything that you do.

CHALLENGE:

- Circle the actions that others say you demonstrate consistently.

- Place an X beside those actions you are not demonstrating consistently at this time.
- Place a box around the number in the growth matrix that best represents where you are today in your growth journey.
- Identify one action that you want to pursue in order to grow in this area.

UNPRODUCTIVE	PRODUCTIVE	ACCOMPLISHED
1	2 3	4
• I don't value planning to make decisions; I mostly rely on my feelings at the time. • I view timing as something out of my control. • I blame others when timing doesn't work out to benefit me.	• I value planning and associated research before making a decision. • I invite those that have a vested interest in the outcome to weigh into my options before I make a decision. • I evaluate the outcomes of my decisions with a desire to learn from my successes and my failures.	• I evaluate and rate my performance related to timing on a consistent basis. • I have an expert team in place that I leverage for decision-making input to improve my timing. • I always own up to the responsibility for the decisions that I make, and their associated outcomes, and learn from them.

5

OVERCOME

OVERCOMING IS NECESSARY to win in any environment that you participate in. In sports, overcoming physical and emotional setbacks are part of the path for those that want to compete at the highest levels. Those that were impacted by adversity in their youth, or those impacted by an unexpected tragedy in their adult years, have to overcome their circumstances or risk staying a victim the rest of their lives. For some, they've made bad life or business decisions and have to deal with the consequences of those decisions.

Puja had to overcome the sudden death of her father and learn to focus on the positive, and Dilpreet needed to overcome a family mindset by pushing through to attain her dreams. Many people have an inherent capability, something that they seem to be born with, that motivates them to overcome difficult circumstances mostly on their own. I see this in both Puja and Dilpreet.

There are many of us, on the other hand, that need help to overcome. The goal is to work through it, not push it down and cover it up. If you don't overcome your difficult situations, most likely they will stunt your growth personally and professionally over time. There is always a way to overcome. It may take longer than you planned, and it might take you on a seemingly unchartered path, but it will be worth the journey if you are willing to ask for help.

CHALLENGE:

- Circle the actions that others say you demonstrate consistently.
- Place an X beside those actions you are not demonstrating consistently at this time.
- Place a box around the number in the growth matrix that best represents where you are today in your growth journey.
- Identify one action that you want to pursue in order to grow in this area.

<table>
<tr><th colspan="2">UNPRODUCTIVE</th><th colspan="2">PRODUCTIVE</th><th colspan="2">ACCOMPLISHED</th></tr>
<tr><td>1</td><td colspan="2">2</td><td colspan="2">3</td><td>4</td></tr>
<tr><td colspan="2">• I push every hardship down inside of me to give the appearance that I am always okay.
• I don't have close friends and colleagues that I let into my personal life.
• I feel like a victim and blame people and circumstances for my present situation.</td><td colspan="2">• I understand that difficult situations will come my way and I embrace the challenge to overcome.
• I have trusted friends and colleagues that will give me honest insights and advice when my circumstances are overwhelming to me.
• I embrace a constructive path forward to overcome and take full personal responsibility for my actions.</td><td colspan="2">• I embrace adversity with a proven method that has worked for me over time.
• I have an expert team that supports my overcoming lifestyle (financial, complex business issues, spiritual, interpersonal relationships, etc.).
• I offer myself as a mentor to those that have a difficult time overcoming their circumstances.</td></tr>
</table>

6

EXCELLENCE

I THINK YOU CAN agree with me that when you experience excellence in something—whether it's an amazing meal prepared to perfection, the taste of an age-old wine that leaves you speechless, or a speaker that brings you to a moment of crystal-clear clarity regarding your present situation—you have to admit that when that moment occurs, you absolutely know that you have just experienced something very special.

Puja and Dilpreet bring excellence into the marketplace with the intent to help leaders make better strategic decisions. In doing so, they keep their eyes on the global market so that their approach, delivery, and presentation support the overall value chain of decision-making while continually adapting and adding value as times change. Bringing excellence into the marketplace today isn't just performing a task perfectly; it's bringing your entire "A-Game" forward in a way that brings significant overall value to your client. It's providing your contribution and also anticipating how it connects to other parts of an overall client solution, the marketplace, and even your community.

CHALLENGE:

- Circle the actions that others say you demonstrate consistently.

- Place an X beside those actions you are not demonstrating consistently at this time.
- Place a box around the number in the growth matrix that best represents where you are today in your growth journey.
- Identify one action that you want to pursue in order to grow in this area.

UNPRODUCTIVE	PRODUCTIVE	ACCOMPLISHED
1	2 3	4
• I base excellence on my best efforts. • I don't think about how my products and services add value to my clients in a tangible way. • I only receive personal and professional insights from people that like me.	• I base excellence on proven industry standards that are valued by my customers. • I receive candid feedback from my clients on my performance every time I do a transaction with them. • I stay connected with the market via market research, industry events, and conferences to make sure that I am providing differentiated value to my clients.	• I seek and receive insights on market trends and current events personally from senior leaders in my industry. • I have regular interactions with my most senior client leaders to understand how I can serve them well in the future. • My personal goal is to see my products and services set the standard in the marketplace for excellence.

7

RESOLVE

EARLIER IN MY career, when I had a complex situation that I was trying to bring resolution to, I would ask my boss at the time what I should do. I laid out all the facts that I had at the time. Being the jokester that he was, he would say with all the conviction that he could muster up, "I feel strongly both ways!" and then laugh. We would then break everything down and he would give me his opinion, but tell me that it was my decision and that I needed to own the end result. I took that to heart, and exercising that wisdom has served me well over the years.

Puja and Dilpreet didn't know how everything was going to work out when they dove into starting their own company. What I love about their approach is that they trusted what was welling up inside of them, had great resolve about their plan, and didn't analyze everything to death. I also appreciate that they didn't try to get someone else to make the decision for them, thus creating an open door to blame that person if things didn't turn out as they planned. The last thing that I appreciate is when they made their choice, they moved forward and never looked back. How many times have we beat ourselves up on a decision when things got tough, instead of just pushing through until we breakthrough?

CHALLENGE:

- Circle the actions that others say you demonstrate consistently.
- Place an X beside those actions you are not demonstrating consistently at this time.
- Place a box around the number in the growth matrix that best represents where you are today in your growth journey.
- Identify one action that you want to pursue in order to grow in this area.

<table>
<tr><th colspan="2">UNPRODUCTIVE</th><th colspan="2">PRODUCTIVE</th><th colspan="2">ACCOMPLISHED</th></tr>
<tr><td>1</td><td colspan="2">2</td><td colspan="2">3</td><td>4</td></tr>
<tr><td colspan="2">• I don't completely commit to strategic areas of focus because I don't want to miss out on new opportunities that come along.
• I consistently second-guess strategic decisions when I start to see resistance to accomplishing them.
• I blame others when things go wrong.</td><td colspan="2">• I commit to strategic areas of focus and take responsibility for my actions to see things come to life.
• I focus on results when things get tough so that I don't second-guess myself and lose my momentum.
• If I get to the end of the effort and things don't go as planned, I take my learnings, adjust my direction, and move forward with a new plan.</td><td colspan="2">• I have multiple strategic areas of focus in play and I persevere and stay focused on results.
• I anticipate where I will likely experience resistance to success and align extra resources to overcome the obstacles.
• I mentor team members and leaders in exercising grit to achieve their strategic initiatives.</td></tr>
</table>

8

FOCUS

TO STATE THE obvious, there is certainly a lot going on in the world today. Just to state a few, we have wars, rising inflation, significant supply chain disruptions, lack of trust with governments, fuel and food shortages, distrust with the media, and have just overcome a global pandemic. All of these things and more are hitting every region of the world at the same time. How this is impacting each individual is different, but to be sure, it is impacting everyone. In these turbulent times, it's difficult to get focused and stay focused on the tasks at hand.

To help keep your focus, it will be more and more important to make sure that you are committed to the vision that you want to execute. Are you "all in"? Because there is so much information coming at everyone from seemingly every corner of the world, you will have to limit your exposure to only those things that will help you achieve your vision. As we saw with Puja and Dilpreet, when uncertain times came early on, they stayed resolute in their vision, exercised transparency and humility with each other, and leveraged each other's strengths to press through difficult times. Engage with outside industry leaders that can mentor and coach you along the way so that you don't feel isolated in what you are trying to accomplish. Engage daily in something that you enjoy: music, exercise, creative writing, watching old movies, etc. It should be something that brings you pleasure and helps invigorate you on a personal level.

CHALLENGE:

- Circle the actions that others say you demonstrate consistently.
- Place an X beside those actions you are not demonstrating consistently at this time.
- Place a box around the number in the growth matrix that best represents where you are today in your growth journey.
- Identify one action that you want to pursue in order to grow in this area.

UNPRODUCTIVE	PRODUCTIVE	ACCOMPLISHED
1	2 3	4
• I spend over an hour a day in various forms of media that are not related to my strategic areas of focus. • I talk about my fears and concerns continuously when turbulent times come to see if someone can help tame my emotions. • I allow my mind to focus on my problems without rest.	• I focus my attention on media that connects me to more insights to achieve my goals. • When I am uneasy with turbulent times, I seek insights from trusted friends who are also committed to staying focused on achieving their goals. • I understand that I need to refresh myself and engage in things that give me joy, like sports, hobbies, family, and being creative in artistic expressions.	• I network with market shapers in and out of my industry to experience how they focus and overcome. • I have a seasoned work-life balance that fills me up so that I can apply myself to staying focused and overcoming. • I demonstrate a lifestyle of winning to where others seek me out for advice on how to stay focused and overcome.

9
HUMILITY

HAVE YOU HAD the privilege of working with a leader that walks in humility? If you have, you probably had a great experience and grew a lot personally and professionally. I believe a humble leader creates a platform of trust among their team members while setting a high bar for individual contribution and overall team excellence. They are learning and growing with the team and they are not intimidated by surrounding themselves with strong future leaders. They don't have to be the smartest person in the room, and as a result, they are focused on harvesting the best ideas from team members and publicly recognizing great individual effort.

Puja and Dilpreet bring these qualities to bare in their leadership style. It's never about them; it's about the success of the overall mission of the company. They surround themselves with world-class team members and leverage their strengths in order to navigate the ever-changing market place and the complexity of global clients, as well as company growth.

CHALLENGE:

- Circle the actions that others say you demonstrate consistently.

- Place an X beside those actions you are not demonstrating consistently at this time.
- Place a box around the number in the growth matrix that best represents where you are today in your growth journey.
- Identify one action that you want to pursue in order to grow in this area.

UNPRODUCTIVE	PRODUCTIVE	ACCOMPLISHED
1	2 3	4
• I manage my work entirely around personal success and getting ahead in life. • I don't give credit to others because that will minimize the attention that I should get for my contributions. • I position myself as an expert in all things and rarely admit that I'm wrong.	• I understand that my contribution is part of a greater effort to make the overall team successful. • In my pursuit to be excellent with my contribution, I understand that I am learning and growing and am open to receiving input from others. • I encourage others with their contribution and am willing to lend a hand when team members are struggling.	• I work daily to set a standard for humility in my environment by focusing on excellent execution while being transparent when I miss the mark. • I surround myself in my environment with strong present and future leaders that are more advanced than me in certain areas to make sure that the best ideas are represented. • I am mentored and/or coached by seasoned professionals to help me remain humble consistently.

10

FEARLESS

WHEN FEAR CONFRONTS us in business, usually from unknown circumstances, there seems to be two general types of reactions to it. The first reaction is to be captivated by it, which will immediately start to hold us back, slow us down, and even paralyze our forward movement. The second reaction is to stay focused on the end goal and see fear as an unknown problem that can be solved.

Everyone has to deal with fear as it comes. It's unavoidable. How you deal with it dictates your future situation. For example, I can be fearless in taking financial risks, but never leave my home for fear of getting sick. I can be fearful to get on an airplane, and be completely fearless in speaking in front of thousands of people. Even though we conquer fear in some areas, there is a high probability that we have to overcome fear in other areas.

What I love about Chris is his general curiosity about life and his appetite for adventure. These two combined elements seem to work together to catapult him forward into a fearless lifestyle. As you read in his story, he has so many "firsts" in his life that when faced with the fear of the unknown, the fear of failure, etc., he excitedly keeps his eyes on the end goal, which allows him to keep his head down and keep working through his situation in order to pierce the darkness that fear can bring.

CHALLENGE:

- Circle the actions that others say you demonstrate consistently.
- Place an X beside those actions you are not demonstrating consistently at this time.
- Place a box around the number in the growth matrix that best represents where you are today in your growth journey.
- Identify one action that you want to pursue in order to grow in this area.

UNPRODUCTIVE	PRODUCTIVE	ACCOMPLISHED
1	2 3	4
• I don't like to take risks and I always play it safe with my personal and professional life. • When asked to take on more responsibility at work, I decline due to the fear of failure or of complicating my life. • I caution others against their passions, goals, and dreams for fear of disappointment.	• I intentionally take on personal and professional goals that stretch me beyond my comfort level. • When confronted by an unknown situation, I purpose to resist fear and rely on my experience, training, and advice from others to overcome. • I encourage others in my environment to take risks and embrace unknowns in order to pursue their passions, goals, and dreams.	• I have a history of success of overcoming fear and I foster a culture of fearlessness that inspires others. • I am continuously pursuing new opportunities that involve levels of risk and associated reward. • I have a network of fearless people that surround me and encourage me to grow in overcoming unknowns in order to succeed in my passions, goals, and dreams.

11

SEE

IN A LARGE city, within a large office building, I had a horrible experience in a meeting where I was attacked verbally by a superior without cause. I was personally shaken but pushed everything deep down inside until I could get outside and get some fresh air. I gathered my things and hopped on a packed elevator to make my way down to the ground floor. I didn't look at anyone; I just stared at the floor. As I got off the elevator, an unknown person tapped me on the arm and asked if I was okay. I could barely respond, but that individual took the time to wish me well and then they disappeared into the crowd. In a brief moment, that person was able to see that I was in pain and offered some relief.

With constant pressure and expectations, it's easy to become numb to those around us. Even with people that we work with or encounter regularly, it's easy to only see the role that they perform in our lives, and not see the actual person that is performing the role. As we reflect back to Chris' story, it helps us better understand the importance of getting to know the people around us in a genuine way. It helps us understand their personal journey, what motivates them, and what obstacles they have overcome. The more that we connect with those around us, the more we can support others and also become more enriched in our own journey.

CHALLENGE:

- Circle the actions that others say you demonstrate consistently.
- Place an X beside those actions you are not demonstrating consistently at this time.
- Place a box around the number in the growth matrix that best represents where you are today in your growth journey.
- Identify one action that you want to pursue in order to grow in this area.

<table>
<tr><th colspan="2">UNPRODUCTIVE</th><th colspan="2">PRODUCTIVE</th><th colspan="2">ACCOMPLISHED</th></tr>
<tr><td colspan="1">1</td><td colspan="2">2</td><td colspan="2">3</td><td colspan="1">4</td></tr>
<tr><td colspan="2">• I tend to see others only for the role that they perform in my life.
• If people don't add value to me in my present situation, I see them as irrelevant.
• I invest in people when I can get something out of it for me.</td><td colspan="2">• I purpose to see all individuals as unique and valuable regardless of the role that they represent in my life.
• When teaming with others, I believe and support the fact that every team member adds significant value regardless of their experience, education, or rank.
• I invest in others freely, recognizing that many have invested in me to make me the success that I am today.</td><td colspan="2">• I take time regularly to connect personally with someone that I don't know well, or at all.
• When the situation arises, I take time to help support those that have been mistreated in life.
• I financially support, on a monthly basis, non-profit organizations that help others achieve their full personal and professional potential.</td></tr>
</table>

12

LISTEN

I WAS IN A meeting with a very well-known senior leader of a major corporation. It was the first time that I had met with him, so I didn't exactly know what to expect. As we covered the topics of the discussion, I noticed that he was engaged in the meeting so much that he wasn't taking notes. He seemed to absorb all of the information from each topic. As the meeting came to a close, he stated the key topics that were presented and gave his comments with an associated list of detailed next steps. This made such an impression on me because my meeting was at 5:00pm, and he had attended back-to-back meetings that started ten hours earlier... and his next meeting was a board of directors meeting prior to releasing their quarterly earnings to the public.

Distractions, preconceived judgments, pressure to "make something happen," or sometimes not bringing our "A-Game" to work that day can cause us to miss out on so much. What I like about Chris' example is that he practices being present and listening in each encounter that he has. It might be solving a complex business problem, communicating with the waitstaff in a restaurant, or brainstorming on how to improve the socio-economic conditions in a third-world country, but he is always engaged. As a result, he is able to mine so many valuable insights out of his interactions, which helps him in every area of his life.

CHALLENGE:

- Circle the actions that others say you demonstrate consistently.

- Place an X beside those actions you are not demonstrating consistently at this time.
- Place a box around the number in the growth matrix that best represents where you are today in your growth journey.
- Identify one action that you want to pursue in order to grow in this area.

UNPRODUCTIVE	PRODUCTIVE		ACCOMPLISHED
1	2	3	4
• When I'm in a conversation, instead of listening to the other person, I'm thinking about what I'm going to say next. • I listen more intently to the people that I think can help me get ahead in life. • I get impatient and interrupt people when they don't get to the point as quickly as I'd like them to.	• I listen to each person by staying focused and also silencing the alerts on my electronic devices. • I value people by listening to them, regardless of how I perceive their importance, because I know that I can learn valuable lessons from anyone. • When I think that a discussion is getting off track and it's my time to speak, I respectfully ask a question of clarification to help confirm that we are using our time constructively.		• When I have planned meetings with people, I take a brief moment before each interaction to make sure that I understand the goal and intent of the meeting. • As I listen to others, I challenge myself to stay engaged without writing notes by committing key topics to memory. • I remain a student of listening by reading articles and books and attending workshops on growing as a communicator.

13

SACRIFICE

MY PARENTS ARE in their mid-eighties now. Being born in 1937, they have seen and experienced so much. Whenever they are met with hardship, and they definitely have had their share over the decades, they respond with hard work and sacrifice to make it through. They just focus on the solution, working with what they have and helping others along the way. It seems to be ingrained in their DNA.

I see Chris doing the same while he works to leverage his background and expertise to help others that are less fortunate. As you read his story, you see that Chris opened himself up to taking a trip earlier in his career to help a remote tribe in Africa, and his heart was changed forever. When I contemplate the examples from Chris, as well as from my parents, it forces me to wonder if I am doing enough for others.

CHALLENGE:

- Circle the actions that others say you demonstrate consistently.
- Place an X beside those actions you are not demonstrating consistently at this time.
- Place a box around the number in the growth matrix that best represents where you are today in your growth journey.

- Identify one action that you want to pursue in order to grow in this area.

UNPRODUCTIVE		PRODUCTIVE		ACCOMPLISHED
1	2		3	4
• I don't believe that sacrifice is necessary to gain valuable lessons in life. • If I have to choose to work in a job that I don't like to get ahead or receive supplemental income from the government, I'll choose to receive supplemental income. • I believe that others are required to support me financially so that I can pursue my passions in life.		• I understand that I must sacrifice my personal comfort in order to gain insight that will serve me well in the future, and I do not take the easy way out. • If I have a list of things to do that involve varying levels of difficulty, I choose to do the difficult tasks first. • I have identified people that have sacrificed significantly for their causes and use them as inspiration when my circumstances are difficult.		• I am willing to sacrifice for a cause I believe in, even when others don't understand or find value in it. • I commit my time and money to helping others, even if it means that I have to change my lifestyle to complete my commitments. • At times, I sacrifice privately to support people and causes so that I don't pull the attention away from those in need and inadvertently draw attention to myself.

14

IDENTITY

WHEN I WAS young, my family moved every four or five years in order to support my father's career in sales and marketing in the heavy-duty truck industry. As I was about to start my first day at a new school, I was nervous enough that it got the attention of my mother. She asked, "Are you nervous?" When I said yes, she said that she had just the thing to make me feel better. She said, "Just be yourself!" At the age of 12, I had absolutely no idea what being myself meant. What I came to understand over time is that your identity encompasses the things that are important to you on the inside of your being. It embodies your passions, the things that bring you joy, the gifts that you have, and many other things that are important to you as an individual.

Sarah was able to associate early on with key parts of her identity. Having been connected to her mother and father's artistic lifestyle, and easily relating to it, it gave her a natural space to experiment and discover some key things that were important to her. One primary area that she discovered was how color, fashion, and esthetics can come together to make special spaces and special moments. As we read in Sarah's story, her identity also includes characteristics like leadership, compassion, and entrepreneurialism. It's never one thing that defines us, but it is important to take time to find out what is important to us as a person versus only being identified by what we do.

CHALLENGE:

- Circle the actions that others say you demonstrate consistently.
- Place an X beside those actions you are not demonstrating consistently at this time.
- Place a box around the number in the growth matrix that best represents where you are today in your growth journey.
- Identify one action that you want to pursue in order to grow in this area.

UNPRODUCTIVE	PRODUCTIVE	ACCOMPLISHED
1	2 3	4
• I define my identity by my job, my title, the car I drive, and what I can accomplish. • I only develop areas of myself that contribute to the success of my identity. • I determine others' identities by their outward successes.	• What I do in my job, sports, and hobbies are an outward expression of who I am, but they don't define me. • I define my identity by my passions, the things that bring me joy, and my gifts and talents. • My sense of identity is not affected by others' approval or disapproval of me.	• I make a commitment each year to invest in something new that I've been curious about. • I am purposeful to invest time to learn from people that inspire me and motivate me to strengthen my identity. • I encourage and mentor others in embracing the journey of developing their total self.

15

DREAM

WHEN I WAS young, it was common to get in trouble in school for daydreaming. For some, it was very difficult to focus on school work when the warm sun in early spring was calling you to the playground. I agree that there is a time to dream, and maybe the best time to do that isn't in the middle of math class. As children, it was easy to use our imagination to dream about our future: what we will do and what we will become. Unfortunately, as I grew older, the focus for me seemed to become less about using my imagination and more about being practical with a focus on work and getting ahead. I think that we need a healthy balance of dreaming about our possibilities and applying hard work to bring our dreams into reality.

There is no question that our dreams can impact us in profound ways. What I see in Sarah's story is that she is willing to put plans together, along with hard work and sacrifice, to see her dreams become a reality. To get a vision of what you want your life to be in a certain area, or to see the solution to a problem come to life in your imagination, can significantly impact your destiny. To bring this about, here are two key questions that you can ask yourself: 1) Are you willing to develop the dreamer within yourself? 2) Once you have a dream that you want to pursue, are you willing to put the time, effort, and sacrifice into bringing it to life?

CHALLENGE:

- Circle the actions that others say you demonstrate consistently.
- Place an X beside those actions you are not demonstrating consistently at this time.
- Place a box around the number in the growth matrix that best represents where you are today in your growth journey.
- Identify one action that you want to pursue in order to grow in this area.

UNPRODUCTIVE	PRODUCTIVE	ACCOMPLISHED
1	2 3	4
• I rarely have dreamed about my future; I mostly just did as I was told or what was expected of me. • I grew up with a lot of troubles in my family and I was taught that it isn't practical to dream about your future, that dreams don't come true. • I dream all of the time and I'm hoping that all of my dreams will come true.	• I embrace the dreamer in me and take steps to develop that part of myself. • I take focused time and effort to write the dreams down that I want to develop, and I create practical plans to pursue them. • I select a dream that I want to pursue and begin to execute my plan with an understanding that it will take time, hard work, and sacrifice to bring my dream to life.	• I network with others that are pursuing their dreams with passion and hard work, which encourages me and helps bring creativity to my journey. • I set finances aside on a planned basis to invest in other dreamers and to pursue dreams that I haven't dreamed yet. • I encourage and mentor people that are stuck in their circumstances to develop the dreamer within themselves to help them overcome their difficulties.

16
STAY

WHEN YOU MAKE a strategic decision to go down a certain path, and you find out that on that path you are being confronted with unexpected difficult obstacles and barriers, it forces you to choose to stay on that path or abandon your efforts. Sometimes it's the right call to abandon the effort, but when you decide to stay on the path, it's usually because you have a deep conviction out of your identity. It can be a dream that you are pursing, or it can be because of a moral principle that you believe in, or both of the above. When these things are stirring inside of you, you make a decision to press forward because it's worth the fight to try to overcome and win. When we win, it's a sweet victory! When we lose, we gain key learnings and insights that set us up for success in the future.

I recently watched a full-length biographical feature film from 2008 called, Flash of Genius. The film depicted the true story of Robert William Kerns who patented his intermittent windshield wiper invention on December 1, 1964. He won two patent infringement lawsuits against Ford and Chrysler, but it took him twenty-four years of staying the course to win both battles. From Sarah's story, we see her stay the course and win several times throughout her life as she battled huge unexpected obstacles. At one point with The Fed, for example, she stated that if she knew how much she would have had to overcome, she might not have tried. She stayed the course and watched her dream come to life, which has significantly enhanced Clarkston's downtown.

CHALLENGE:

- Circle the actions that others say you demonstrate consistently.
- Place an X beside those actions you are not demonstrating consistently at this time.
- Place a box around the number in the growth matrix that best represents where you are today in your growth journey.
- Identify one action that you want to pursue in order to grow in this area.

UNPRODUCTIVE	PRODUCTIVE	ACCOMPLISHED
1	2 3	4
• When my circumstances get tough, I fear failure and decide to abandon my pursuits and go do something else. • I find solace by seeking comfort from others that also abandon their plans due to fear of failure. • I blame others for my struggles and don't see anything wrong with my pattern of walking away from my commitments when things are tough.	• I take responsibility for my actions and choose to learn from my successes and my failures. • I understand that sacrifice is part of success and I choose to pursue my passions with a strong determination to push through difficult times. • I remain a student in overcoming by aligning with others that have demonstrated tremendous staying power and have succeeded.	• I have documented successes and failures when I stayed the course, and I leverage these learnings to encourage myself and others. • I identify what holds me back and I choose to confront it as part of my daily routine. • I mentor and encourage others to stay on course when they make the choice to give it all they have to try and win.

17
CREATIVITY

WHEN WE ARE exercising creativity, according to Merriam-Webster, we are bringing things into existence, producing or bringing about by a course of action or behavior, and producing through imaginative skill.

Have you spent time with someone that creates for a living: a sculptor, painter, or musician? It's as if they embraced their creativity when they were young and never let go of it. It's a small percentage of people that will make a living entirely with their creative skills alone, but those that maintain some form of creativity seem to have a fuller life than those that don't.

I heard one person say, "I'm not creative." I personally believe that everyone is creative, some just have an easier time exploring it than others. Sarah provides a great example of infusing her businesses with her creative skills. Doing what she enjoys, she became an influencer on Instagram. Dreaming about bringing a special space to downtown Clarkston led her and James to reimagining a bank building into a sought-out restaurant destination. Creativity establishes a place for us to rest from the cares of the world and it brings about new ideas for us to consider. Maybe what some of us are missing is a bit of creativity in our lives.

CHALLENGE:

- Circle the actions that others say you demonstrate consistently.
- Place an X beside those actions you are not demonstrating consistently at this time.
- Place a box around the number in the growth matrix that best represents where you are today in your growth journey.
- Identify one action that you want to pursue in order to grow in this area.

UNPRODUCTIVE	PRODUCTIVE	ACCOMPLISHED
1	2 3	4
• I don't feel I'm creative and I don't invest time there because I don't see the value in it. • I don't participate in creative activities because it makes me feel uncomfortable. • My view on most issues is black and white and I don't open myself to explore other options or opinions.	• I believe that I'm creative and I invest time to develop my creative interests. • I enjoy creative activities because it is a source of freedom for me where I can imagine the possibility of something or learn something new. • When I'm making a difficult or significant decision, I entertain the ideas of others so that I have a broader view of what is possible.	• I make long-term consistent commitments to invest in my creative gifts. • I understand that regularly engaging in creative activities is a source of adult play that reduces stress and helps refresh and recharge me. • I incorporate creativity in decision-making like brainstorming, modeling, and gaming to help me envision the possibilities of a situation.

18
CULTURE

CULTURE WITHIN BUSINESSES, large and small, is continuing to be a key topic of discussion by senior leaders and employees alike. As market pressures and increasing competition for talent continue to be on the rise globally, there is a greater realization that in order to stabilize productivity and bring employee attrition down, leaders need to foster a culture of trust that promotes inclusion, transparency, and authenticity. Employees have more choices than ever today and many of them are fleeing toxic, unpredictable cultures for healthy ones.

When I look at the Stoll family business culture, one that they have been developing for over fifty years and spans three generations, it is clear to me that they are doing something right. They have adopted and practiced a set of values that enhances the lives of their employees, and as a result, their attrition is low, their performance is high, and they are attracting talent that is setting them up for future success. Dennis Stolls' statement to me says it all: "We truly treat people with honor, respect, dignity, and real love. We truly operate every part of our business in a way that cares for others and allows them to prosper."

CHALLENGE:

- Circle the actions that others say you demonstrate consistently.

- Place an X beside those actions you are not demonstrating consistently at this time.
- Place a box around the number in the growth matrix that best represents where you are today in your growth journey.
- Identify one action that you want to pursue in order to grow in this area.

UNPRODUCTIVE	PRODUCTIVE	ACCOMPLISHED
1	2 3	4
• How I choose to treat others at work is my own business, even if it is disrespectful and dishonoring. • I look the other way when toxic behavior is being demonstrated because it's not my responsibility to get involved. • If I have a concern about the company culture, I keep it to myself and don't bring it up to my leaders to discuss it.	• I understand that my actions toward others impact the company culture and I behave in a way that demonstrates honor and respect of others. • I actively, but tactfully, confront toxic behavior in my environment because I know that it's everyone's responsibility to support a healthy culture. • When I see the culture of my company adopting behaviors that are unproductive, I discuss it with my leaders.	• I investigate and learn what values and principles are involved in establishing a healthy and productive culture and I work as an influencer to bring those things to life. • I mentor future leaders in developing healthy cultures. • I foster an environment of trust and genuine care for the personal and professional success of others in every area of influence that I have.

19
BIG

ONE PHRASE THAT comes to mind when I think of the word big is, "go big or go home." It's the idea that there are times when going after something with everything that you have makes the difference between winning and losing your place for a promotion, your opportunity to enter the market with a unique product, or starting your own business, just to name a few. I find that some of us have a difficult time going big with our efforts because we are thinking too small. 1) We think locally when we should be thinking globally. 2) We spend too much time focusing on our weaknesses instead of leveraging our strengths and capabilities to overcome. 3) We look at the obstacles instead of the opportunities.

In looking at the Stoll family story, what is interesting is that each generation from the very beginning had big dreams. Each generation was willing to step out with the resources that they had in order to pursue them. The first big dream caused the family to move to an unfamiliar state and start a small local business. The second big dream took the small local business to a national business. The third big dream significantly expanded the business into many new market segments by bringing new innovative products to their customers. We can't go big with every idea that we have, but pick the ones that are the most important to you and give it all that you've got!

CHALLENGE:

- Circle the actions that others say you demonstrate consistently.
- Place an X beside those actions you are not demonstrating consistently at this time.
- Place a box around the number in the growth matrix that best represents where you are today in your growth journey.
- Identify one action that you want to pursue in order to grow in this area.

<table>
<tr><th colspan="2">UNPRODUCTIVE</th><th colspan="2">PRODUCTIVE</th><th colspan="2">ACCOMPLISHED</th></tr>
<tr><td>1</td><td colspan="2">2</td><td colspan="2">3</td><td>4</td></tr>
<tr><td colspan="2">• I don't like to dream big because I'd rather keep things small and predictable.
• I have big dreams, but I don't want to expose myself if it doesn't work out.
• I have weaknesses that I need to overcome before I try something big.</td><td colspan="2">• I develop big ideas in key areas because I want to be responsible to challenge myself to reach my full potential.
• I know that pursuing a big idea is bigger than my individual capabilities and resources and I will need the support of others to bring my big idea into reality.
• I am committed to leveraging my strengths and seeing obstacles in my path as opportunities to overcome.</td><td colspan="2">• I invest time and money in developing one big personal idea each year for myself.
• I have a mature decision-making process in place that helps me determine which big ideas I will invest in during this season of life.
• I have a network of people that are also pursuing big ideas and we encourage each other and at times invest in each other's ideas.</td></tr>
</table>

20

TESTED

I'M SURE THAT everyone that is reading this book has most likely been through a job interview of some kind. It's called an interview to make it sound inviting, but as we all know, we are being tested to see if our education aligns with the job specification, do our experiences match the requirements needed to perform the job, can we demonstrate that we've handled and overcome difficult situations, can we confirm that we have specific certifications if required, and more increasingly, do we fit their company culture?

For entrepreneurs, you are also being tested. Your customers are evaluating your products and services every time they encounter them. They are publicly ranking their experiences via social media and giving you instantaneous results. You are being tested on how you respond to an ever-changing market by watching your revenues rise or fall, you are being tested on your operational capabilities by how healthy your balance sheet is, and on and on. Stoll Industries has been tested in all of these areas and more. They have passed yet another test and that's the test of time as they recently celebrated their fiftieth year in business. I think that we can all agree that being tested is a part of life. Do you avoid being tested or do you embrace it as an opportunity to grow and develop?

CHALLENGE:

- Circle the actions that others say you demonstrate consistently.
- Place an X beside those actions you are not demonstrating consistently at this time.
- Place a box around the number in the growth matrix that best represents where you are today in your growth journey.
- Identify one action that you want to pursue in order to grow in this area.

<table>
<tr><th colspan="4">UNPRODUCTIVE</th><th colspan="4">PRODUCTIVE</th><th colspan="4">ACCOMPLISHED</th></tr>
<tr><td colspan="3">1</td><td colspan="3">2</td><td colspan="3">3</td><td colspan="3">4</td></tr>
<tr><td colspan="4">• I avoid being tested at all costs so that I don't have to feel uncomfortable if I don't do well.
• I am okay using other people's work and calling it my own if I can pass the test with flying colors.
• I avoid taking on more responsibility so that I can avoid being tested at higher levels.</td><td colspan="4">• I understand that being tested is part of life, so I embrace the concept with open arms.
• I embrace the challenge and hard work that it takes to bring my authentic self into the marketplace, so I refuse to take someone else's accomplishments as my own for short-term gain.
• I look for opportunities to take on more responsibility so that I can be challenged to grow and develop in my gifts and talents.</td><td colspan="4">• I have a track record of being tested and overcoming, which encourages me to keep pursuing new ideas to bring to the marketplace.
• I remain a student to learn new ideas and concepts, regardless of my rank and experience, so I continue to grow in new areas.
• As I near the end of my career(s), I write my experiences down so I can pass them on to encourage the next generation.</td></tr>
</table>

21

RELEVANT

WHEN YOU ARE positioning a product or service, or trying to convey a thought or a concept, one of the most significant success factors in accomplishing this goal is aligning with the needs and interests of your audience, thus being relevant. As a result of this, individuals and companies go to great lengths to test the market to determine if what they are positioning aligns with the market's needs, and if so, to what degree.

What I see with the leaders at Stoll Industries is that they seem to have been able to put themselves in a place where they challenge themselves to stay relevant in most every key decision that they make. Do they hit the mark every time? Certainly not, but they do position themselves to focus on it within each department. Examples of how they do this are: 1) Listening to the advice of their distributors, customers, and expert coaches. 2) Always being open to ideas from their entire team on how they can operate better as a company. 3) Challenging their teams to come up with creative solutions to bring future products to life. 4) Remaining students that embrace change, making sure that they don't fall into "We've never done it that way" thinking and miss an opportunity to craft a new approach.

CHALLENGE:

- Circle the actions that others say you demonstrate consistently.

- Place an X beside those actions you are not demonstrating consistently at this time.
- Place a box around the number in the growth matrix that best represents where you are today in your growth journey.
- Identify one action that you want to pursue in order to grow in this area.

<table>
<tr><th colspan="4">UNPRODUCTIVE</th><th colspan="4">PRODUCTIVE</th><th colspan="4">ACCOMPLISHED</th></tr>
<tr><td colspan="3">1</td><td colspan="3">2</td><td colspan="3">3</td><td colspan="3">4</td></tr>
<tr><td colspan="4">• I believe that I am the only one that truly understands what my clients need.
• I don't involve other team members or advisors when making decisions about bringing my products and services to the market.
• If I hit the mark and I'm successful, I take full credit, but if I miss the mark and fail, I do not take personal responsibility for the failure.</td><td colspan="4">• I know that the marketplace is multifaceted, and though I have a perspective, I must get candid honest feedback from my clients and my team members in order to hit the mark with my approach.
• I practice being relevant in my conversations by asking if I'm coming across clearly, as I'm more interested in them receiving my thoughts instead of just talking at them.
• I leverage personal coaching and mentoring to help me grow in my interpersonal skills.</td><td colspan="4">• I purpose to have relevant conversations with varying age groups to practice communicating effectively.
• I have an established board of advisors, with varying skill sets and experiences, that help challenge my ideas and approaches to assure that I'm being relevant.
• In seeing what works and doesn't work in my marketplace over time, I have a list of questions that I use to vet ideas before I give them serious consideration.</td></tr>
</table>

APPENDIX

STUDY QUESTIONS

CHAPTER ONE

1. What motivates John McMullen to be an extravagant giver, supporting community initiatives, blood and cancer drives, and individuals in need?
2. How does John McMullen's impeccable timing and focus on operational excellence contribute to his consistent success in investment decisions, dealership transactions, and his automobile collection?
3. In what ways does John McMullen demonstrate his gift for recognizing and selecting great team members throughout his career?

CHAPTER TWO

1. How did Puja and Dilpreet's resilient restart in their first year of business contribute to their success?
2. How do Puja and Dilpreet exemplify the qualities of being givers and servant leaders?

3. How have Puja and Dilpreet demonstrated the characteristics of resilience and determination in their entrepreneurial journey?

CHAPTER THREE

1. What were the key factors that led Chris to step down from his position at Waymo and dedicate himself fully to the Afreecar project?
2. Based on the entrepreneurial insights discussed, how has Chris demonstrated fearlessness, a focus on individuals, listening skills, and a willingness to sacrifice
3. What challenges did Chris face when adapting his initial concept of a small solar-powered trailer for the African market, and how did he overcome them?

CHAPTER FOUR

1. How did Sarah and James approach the process of bidding on the bank building despite being underdogs in the purchasing process?
2. How did Sarah gather information and ideas for the concept and operation of the restaurant, considering her lack of experience in owning and operating such a business?
3. How did Sarah's experience of dealing with critiques and feedback from customers shape her approach to running The Fed and improving their operations?

CHAPTER FIVE

1. How has the Stoll family's approach of honoring and respecting suppliers contributed to their supply chain resilience during disruptions?
2. How does Stoll Industries' culture of honor and respect foster a healthy work environment and strong relationships with employees, suppliers, and customers?
3. How do the Stolls' dreams and actions drive the growth and success of Stoll Industries, and how do they stay relevant in the market?

PART 2 STUDY QUESTIONS

1. How do fear, empty promises, and self-centered approaches hinder a leader's ability to gain respect?
2. What are the key attributes of a high-performing team?
3. How did John McMullen exemplify the attributes of a giver?
4. Why is timing crucial in decision-making?
5. Why is overcoming adversity important for growth?
6. How has the concept of excellence evolved in the marketplace?
7. How did Puja and Dilpreet demonstrate resolve in starting their own company?
8. How can individuals maintain focus amidst distractions?
9. How do Puja and Dilpreet embody humility in their leadership style?
10. How does fear impact decision-making in business?

11. Reflect on Chris's example of getting to know people on a genuine level. How can this practice benefit us in various aspects of life?
12. How do distractions and preconceived judgments hinder effective listening?
13. In what ways can we evaluate if we are doing enough for others and make adjustments to our actions?
14. How does understanding and embracing our identity contribute to personal fulfillment and well-being?
15. What are the key factors that determine whether dreams remain mere fantasies or become tangible achievements?
16. What lessons can be learned from Robert William Kerns' perseverance in the face of long-term setbacks?
17. How does incorporating creativity into different aspects of life contribute to overall satisfaction?
18. Reflect on a positive or negative workplace culture experience and its impact on motivation and productivity.
19. Describe a personal experience where you took a big risk or pursued a significant dream. What challenges did you encounter, and what did you learn?
20. Reflect on a testing situation, such as a job interview or evaluation of your products/services. How did you respond, and what did you learn?
21. How can actively seeking feedback from customers, team members, and industry experts help in staying relevant and meeting market needs?

Index

H

I

J

K

L

M

N

O

P

Q

R

S

T

U

V

W

Y

ACKNOWLEDGEMENTS

This book became a reality because five entrepreneurs gave me permission to tell their stories. I am forever changed by their vision, passion, grit, humility and market place impact. Their stories are forever imprinted in my mind and in my heart. Thank you, John McMullen, Puja Bhattacharya, Dilpreet Chadha, Chris Borroni-Bird, Sarah Schneider and the Stoll family.

With this being my first book project, I had a vision of what I wanted to accomplish, but I didn't have an understanding of what was involved in bringing it into reality. David Sluka became my coach and guided me throughout the process. He challenged me, inspired me, and believed in me. David, I am, and will be forever grateful for all that you have done to help me bring this project to completion.

Thank you, Nick Poe with Tall Pine Books, for embracing my vision for this project and for bringing perfect clarity in finalizing the title. Thank you, Yvonne Parks for designing the book cover with passion and excellence.

Lastly, thank you Mary Childers, my amazing sister, for agreeing to meet with me weekly to pray for this project. Your love, encouragement, and insight made a significant impact on me and on this book project.

MEET THE AUTHOR

PATRICK O'MEARA, located in Clarkston, Michigan with his wife, Rosella and daughter, Annalise, is the founder of Growth Matrix, LLC, a global services organization that helps individuals and companies realize and achieve their potential.

For the last thirty-three years, he has been a senior leader within global services, software, and business consulting companies, and has served some of the largest and most complex corporations in the world. Patrick has led strategic international delivery projects where the team members performed as one global unit exceeding anticipated targeted results.

Over his career, he has managed a portfolio of business services spanning IT, finance, operations, talent, and organizational transformation.

He has advised software and services executives, and board of management teams, around mergers and acquisitions and initial public offering activities on growth initiatives within the United States and Europe.

GrowthMatrixLLC.com

www.ingramcontent.com/pod-product-compliance
Lightning Source LLC
Chambersburg PA
CBHW031846090426
42741CB00005B/380

* 9 7 8 1 9 5 5 5 4 6 3 9 3 *